SPIRITUAL
TRADITIONS

Essential Teachings to Transform Your Life

SPIRITUAL TRADITIONS

Essential Teachings to Transform Your Life

TIMOTHY FREKE

Sterling Publishing Co., Inc.
New York

This Book is Dedicated to You

Library of Congress Cataloging-in-Publication
Data Available

10 9 8 7 6 5 4 3 2 1

Published in 2001 by
Sterling Publishing Company, Inc.
387 Park Avenue South, New York, N.Y. 10016
© 2000 Godsfield Press
Text © 2000 Timothy Freke

Timothy Freke asserts the moral right to be
identified as the author of this work.

Distributed in Canada by Sterling Publishing
c/o Canadian Manda Group,
One Atlantic Avenue,
Suite 105, Toronto, Ontario, Canada M6K 3E7
Distributed in Australia by Capricorn Link
(Australia) Pty Ltd, P O. Box 6651, Baulkham
Hills, Business Centre, NSW 2153, Australia

Printed and bound in China

ISBN 0–8069–9844–X

First edition in paperback 2000

Originally published in hardcover as
Encyclopedia of Spirituality.

Introduction 8

PART ONE **SPIRITUAL TRADITIONS** 10

PART TWO **SPIRITUAL PRACTICES** 50

PART THREE **SPIRITUAL TEACHINGS** 148

PART FOUR **INFORMATION AT A GLANCE** 246

Introduction

W*HAT'S IT ALL ABOUT? Why am I here? Who am I? Is there a God? How should I live? What is death? At some time or other most of us have felt overwhelmed by such profound questions. Spirituality is about exploring these fundamental enigmas. Although in the past spirituality has usually been associated with organized religion, it is not necessarily religious. To embark on the spiritual quest for meaning is a natural human response to a mysterious life.*

SEARCHING FOR ANSWERS

BECOMING A PSYCHONAUT

Science, the dominant philosophy of the modern age, has taught us a great deal about how life works, but remains dumb when faced with the question of why life is and what we should be doing with it. Such questions cannot be answered by using scientific methods, but only by exploring the inner world of imagination and intuitive insight. Our exploration of the physical universe has given us the power to send astronauts into outer space, but to penetrate the profound mysteries of existence each one of us must become a "psychonaut" and make a personal journey into the inner space of consciousness.

INFORMATION AND INSPIRATION

We live in extraordinary times. Unlike other periods in history, we are not compelled to express our spirituality in the dominant form adopted by our culture. The wisdom of all the great spiritual traditions of the world is available for us to study and learn from. Drawing on these spiritual riches, this encyclopedia explores the perennial teachings and practices found at the heart of all the great religions. It is not concerned with customs and dogmas, but with presenting the information and inspiration we need to set off on our own spiritual adventure of discovery.

PRECIOUS WISDOM

This encyclopedia does not contain a curriculum that must be followed. Although it will reward being read from cover to cover, it is designed to allow you to choose and explore those particular teachings and practices that you personally feel drawn to. It is not a comprehensive spiritual system. It is a distillation of some of the precious wisdom passed down by countless mystics and visionaries who have made the spiritual journey before us. Above all it is a practical manual that, if approached with an inquisitive mind and an open heart, can help us transform our ordinary lives into an extraordinary journey of awakening.

TO BOLDLY GO ...

Traditions, Practices, and Teachings

Part One

The first section of this book explores the major spiritual traditions and their different philosophies, and investigates what is happening to spirituality today.

Part Two

The second section examines traditional spiritual practices that have been used by pilgrims for centuries and suggests simple ways we can try out these techniques for ourselves.

Part Three

The third section focuses on the perennial teachings found at the heart of all spiritual traditions and how we can apply them in our own lives.

Part Four

The fourth section contains a glossary and index to provide a quick reference to some of the terms and ideas outlined in this book.

PART ONE

PART TWO

PART THREE

PART FOUR

❝ Before enlightenment,

Buddhas are no different than ordinary people.

After enlightenment,

ordinary people at once become Buddhas. ❞

HUI-NENG
ZEN MASTER

❝ If you have a heart, you can be saved. ❞

ABBA PAMBO
CHRISTIAN SAGE

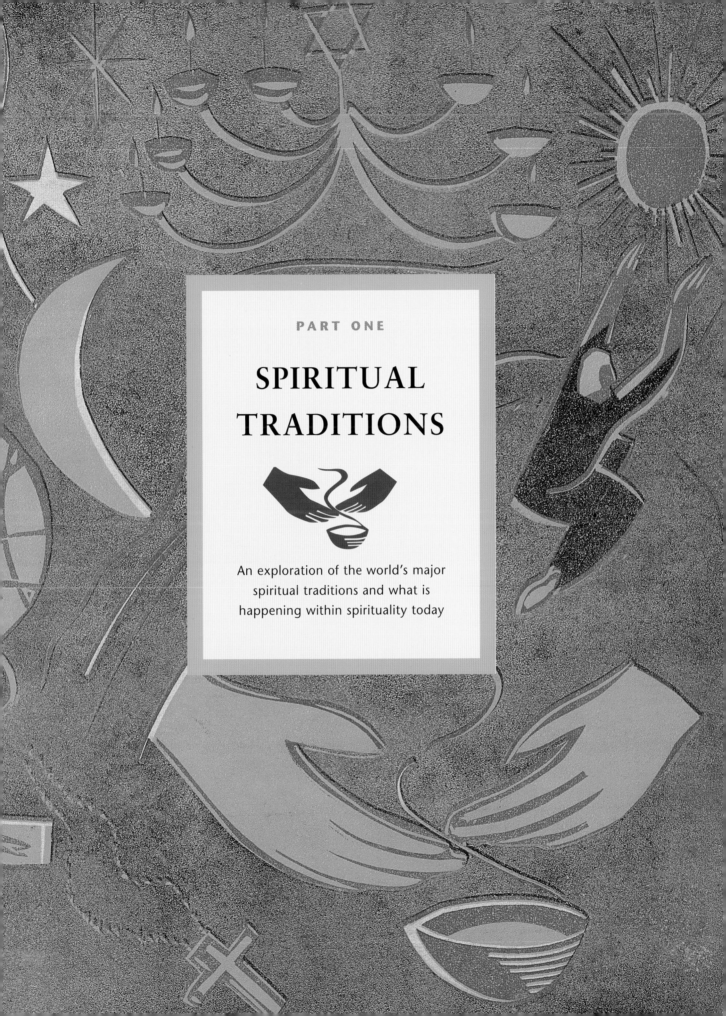

PART ONE

SPIRITUAL
TRADITIONS

An exploration of the world's major
spiritual traditions and what is
happening within spirituality today

SPIRITUAL TRADITIONS

T*HIS SECTION OF THE book explores the world's major spiritual traditions and what is happening within spirituality today. Spiritual traditions can be divided into those with polytheistic, monotheistic, and monist philosophies. Polytheistic traditions,*

such as Shamanism, Hinduism, and ancient Paganism, believe in many gods and goddesses. Monotheistic traditions,

PREHISTORIC
GODDESS

such as Judaism, Christianity, and Islam, believe in one God. Monist traditions, such as Taoism and Buddhism, believe in an impersonal Oneness. Although these traditions sound very different, in fact they share a great deal in common.

A HINDU YOGI'S
VISION OF GOD

A PAGAN GODDESS,
PAINTED BY
GIOVANNI SEGANTINI

Touching the Elephant

Some Indians kept an elephant in a dark room. Because it was impossible to see the elephant, those that wanted to know something about this exotic beast had to feel it with their hands. The first person went into the darkness and felt the elephant's trunk and announced, "This creature is like a water-pipe." The next person felt the elephant's ear and asserted, "No. It's like a giant fan."

A third person felt the elephant's leg and declared, "That's not true. This animal resembles a pillar." A fourth person felt the elephant's back and concluded, "Not at all. It's like a throne." Different points of view produce different opinions. If someone had brought in a candle, they would've all felt like fools.

SUFI TEACHING STORY

MONOTHEISM AND POLYTHEISM

These divisions of spiritual traditions are helpful to a point, but they have also been the cause of much misunderstanding and confusion, leading to an unnecessary sense of fundamental conflict between these philosophies. For example, polytheists are often condemned by monotheists for believing in many divinities and not comprehending that there is only one Supreme Being. Actually, however, polytheistic traditions teach that there is ultimately one God. Indeed they teach that essentially all is One. The Native Americans call this supreme unity "Great Spirit" or "Great Mystery." The Hindus know it as "Brahman." The ancient Pagan philosophers knew it simply as "the One" or "the Good."

FACES OF THE FACELESS

This One God of the polytheistic traditions embraces everything and cannot be identified with any particular qualities or characteristics. It can, therefore, seem abstract and unapproachable. The various gods and goddesses are faces of the faceless sublime Oneness; personas with recognizably human characteristics that the impersonal Oneness adopts so that we can have a personal relationship with it. In ancient Egypt the "gods" were called "neters," from which, via Latin, some scholars believe we get our word "nature." The neters are expressions of the many natures of the One Nature of the Supreme Being.

UNDERLYING UNITY

Monism, polytheism, and monotheism are actually all remarkably similar. Monist traditions believe in an impersonal Oneness. Polytheism, likewise, is ultimately concerned with an ineffable God without attributes. And the great mystics of Judaism, Christianity, and Islam also point to a transcendental unity, beyond the idea of a personal God, sometimes called the Godhead.

Just as polytheism worships the one God via a pantheon of lesser deities, monotheism worships its one God via a hierarchy of angelic beings, saints, and prophets, and, in practice, Monist traditions also recognize a whole host of gods, celestial Buddhas, and nature spirits.

MANY RIVERS TO ONE SEA

The different spiritual traditions of the world are unique expressions of common themes. They are different rivers running to one sea of Truth. Each tradition has its own way of seeing reality, its own conceptual language, its cultural biases, its particular history, and its own great saints and sages. Each tradition, therefore, has something valuable to offer us in our exploration of the mysteries of life and death.

THE ANCIENT EGYPTIAN DEITIES
HORUS, OSIRIS, AND ISIS

ALL PHILOSOPHIES ARE INADEQUATE

Yet the enlightened masters of all traditions teach that the ultimate Truth is beyond the scope of words ever to express. All spiritual philosophies are only gestures toward the inexpressible. As such they are all partially valid and all ultimately inadequate. As the Hindu sage Mahatma Gandhi writes:

SPANISH FRIAR DISCOURSING WITH MUSLIMS, C.1600

MAHATMA GANDHI

"Religions are different roads converging on the same point. What does it matter that we take different roads so long as we reach the same goal? I believe that all religions of the world are true more or less. I say 'more or less' because I believe that everything the human hand touches, by reason of the very fact that human beings are imperfect, becomes imperfect."

Fundamentalism and Mysticism

A spiritual tradition is rarely homogeneous, but is in reality made up of people with widely different levels of spiritual understanding. This ranges from religious fundamentalists to enlightened mystics. Fundamentalists are concerned with differentiating their beliefs from those of others, while mystics are ultimately unconcerned with beliefs and dogmas and emphasize understanding the underlying unity of all things. While fundamentalists are implacably hostile to other traditions, mystics recognize other traditions as different roads up the same mountain of Truth.

What Color Is a Chameleon?

Three men went into the jungle on different occasions and saw a chameleon. "A chameleon is red," said the first man. "No, a chameleon is green," said the second man. "Nonsense, a chameleon is brown," said the the third man. Those who disagree about the nature of God are like these three men.

HINDU TEACHING STORY

RELIGIOUS TOLERANCE

The various deities of polytheism are different masks of the ineffable God. They allow people of different temperaments to approach the ultimate Being via a face that they find appealing. In India, for example, one person may worship Vishnu, the preserver of life, through song and devotion. Another may follow Shiva, the destroyer of illusion, through the path of asceticism and meditation. Both the worshiper of Vishnu and of Shiva, however, reach through their adopted deity toward the same faceless supreme God. This encourages a profound sense of religious tolerance.

The myths told of the gods and goddesses superficially appear to be just popular folktales, but they are often also sophisticated allegories of the process of spiritual awakening or imaginative expositions of metaphysical theories. It is easy to dismiss the gods and goddesses as fantastical illusions, but polytheistic traditions treat them as perfectly real spirit beings. Yet they also teach that, on a higher level, all separate beings are illusionary, including the gods and goddesses. In reality everything is an aspect of the One Supreme Being.

MUSLIMS AT DAWN PRAYERS DURING THE HOLY MONTH OF RAMADAN

66 Truth is One and the learned call it by many names. **99**

RG VEDA
HINDU SCRIPTURE

ॐॐॐॐ

66 There is one river of Truth that receives tributaries from every side. **99**

CLEMENT OF ALEXANDRIA
CHRISTIAN SAINT

ॐॐॐॐ

66 The one doctrine upon which all the world is united is that there is one God who is king of all and father. **99**

MAXIMUS OF TYRE
PAGAN SAGE

ॐॐॐॐ

66 God is not limited to the way he appears to you by making Himself appropriate to your ability to receive Him. Therefore, no one else is obliged to obey the God you worship, for He appears to them in other forms. **99**

IBN ARABI
SUFI SAGE

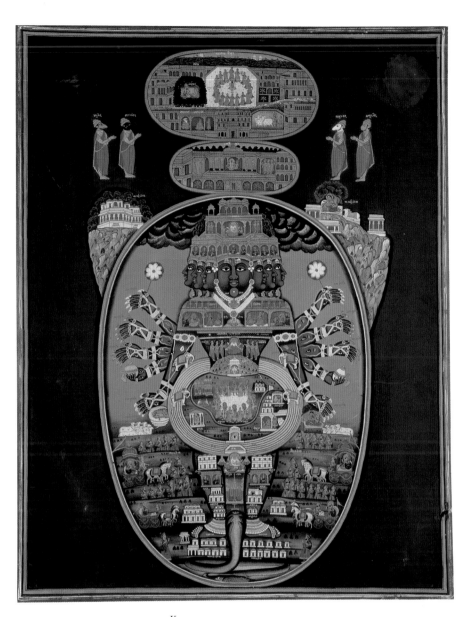

KRISHNA IN COSMIC FORM

A SHAMAN TAKES A HALLUCINOGENIC JOURNEY

Shamanism

S HAMANISM IS THE primal spirituality of our ancestors. Shamanic traditions once flourished all over the world – from the winter wastelands of Siberia to the open outbacks of Australia, from the tropical jungles of the Amazon to the verdant meadows of Britain. Despite horrific persecution, Shamanism is still practiced by about 200–300 million indigenous peoples today and is becoming increasingly popular in the modern world among those searching for their ancient roots. At its foundation is the understanding that everything exists as a part of one intimately interrelated Web of Life.

A FEMALE SHAMAN

NATURE

The modern world treats Nature as a brute resource to be coerced into fulfilling our insatiable appetites. Shamanism views Nature as the manifest form of Spirit. Everything is alive and conscious in its own way – even the rocks and stones. The Earth is often pictured as a Great Mother from whose abundance all life arises. Shamans are people with a special gift for communing with Nature and communicating with the different forms of consciousness that animate it – the spirits. Shamans are often treated with fear and suspicion because they are seen as more linked to Nature than to the tribe.

A RUSSIAN SHAMAN DRESSED IN ANIMAL SKINS

THE SHAMAN

Shamans induce altered states of awareness by conducting sacred rituals, communing with Nature, ingesting psychedelic power plants, using magical language, singing sacred songs, drumming, and playing music. Once in an altered state, the shaman is able to heal sickness, have visions of where the game is to be found, seek out solutions to personal or tribal problems, and cast light on the meaning of human existence.

THE SPIRITS

Shamanism teaches that the world is permeated by spirits who directly impact on human life and without whose help we could not survive. The shaman is able to communicate with these spirits who control fertility, the weather, and all the other processes that make life possible. The spirits are the source of all that we need, but they in turn need to be fed with offerings of human artifacts and prayers. When this symbiotic relationship between the spirits and humanity has been broken, usually through human forgetfulness, the shaman is called in to restore harmony between the worlds. Many Shamans today explain that neglecting this fundamental relationship with the spirits has caused the spirits to demand their sustenance in ways harmful to human beings, causing new diseases, natural catastrophes, and other modern problems.

THE ANCESTORS

Most Shamanic traditions honor the ancestors – the generations of human beings that connect the tribe back to the primal ancestors, who are often worshiped as gods. Through the primal ancestors this lineage reaches back to the Earth Mother and the Creator God. The ancestors are not dead, but alive in the spirit world. Here they look after their descendants. But in return, they need to be ritually fed and cared for by the living. Unpropitiated ancestral ghosts can become dangerous. They maraud in search of sustenance, often taking possession of a vulnerable member of the family and causing illness.

DRUMMING ALTERS A SHAMAN'S AWARENESS

f Us Australian Aboriginal people, we live in the spirit world more than we do in the living. We depend more on the spirits to guide us than anything outside. "

LORRAINE MAFI-WILLIAMS
ABORIGINAL ELDER

f The goal of Shamanism is to merge totally and completely your spirit within the Whole. "

JAMIE SAMS
NATIVE AMERICAN TEACHER

WORSHIPERS SING TO THE EARTH MOTHER AT A SUMMER SOLSTICE GODDESS FESTIVAL

Hinduism

HINDUISM IS ROOTED *in the ancient Vedas, the oldest sacred writings of humanity. Yet, despite its great age, Hinduism remains a vibrant living tradition, still producing exceptional saints and sages today. It is a broad and inclusive religion made up of many cults that, although they perform different spiritual practices and even propound contradictory philosophies, are all understood as approaches to the one transcendent Truth. This is why the Indians call their faith simply the "santana dharma" – the eternal doctrine. In recent decades Hinduism has had a profound influence on spirituality in the West.*

VISHNU AS
THE WORLD

JIVA, ATMAN, AND BRAHMAN

The essential teaching of Hinduism is that the "jiva" – the individual personal self – is not our true identity. Through spiritual practice we can realize our true identity as the Atman or Higher Self. Through further spiritual awakening we can come to the enlightened realization that "Atman is Brahman" – the Self is God. Our consciousness is an expression of the one Consciousness of the Universe.

KRISHNA WITH HIS MISTRESS, RADHA

YOGA

Hinduism teaches various spiritual paths toward enlightenment known as "yogas." The most important yogas are Bhakti and Gnana. Gnana is often associated with the god Shiva. It is a path of the head that emphasizes philosophical understanding, meditation, and the study of scripture. Through this path seekers understand that the world is an illusion, that they have no individual identity, and that in truth God is all that exists. Bhakti is a path of the heart that emphasizes worship, prayer, and surrender to God. Bhaktas lose themselves in all-consuming ecstatic devotion to God, until they transcend their separate identities and become one with their Beloved. Although the paths of Bhakti Yoga and Gnana Yoga are quite different in approach, their essential purpose is identical – to nurture a spontaneous experience of enlightenment.

THE BLIND MAN AND THE LAME MAN

Someone who practices only Bhakti Yoga is sometimes compared to a blind man who cannot see where to go and so, in his enthusiasm, wanders off in the wrong direction. Someone who practices only Gnana Yoga, on the other hand, is compared to a lame man who can see the distant destination but, because his knowledge is so abstract, makes no progress toward it. Most gurus recommend combining the love and energy of Bhakti Yoga with the wisdom and discrimination of Gnana Yoga.

THE GURU

The guru is a central figure in Hinduism. "Guru" means "one who leads from darkness to light." The true guru has merged his or her individual self with God, so devotees often devote themselves to their guru as a living embodiment of God. An enlightened guru acts as mirror in which devotees can glimpse their own true divine nature. Hindus believe that simply being in the presence of such a being can bring the seeker into a heightened state of awareness – a practice called "darshan."

> " That which we call the Hindu religion is really the eternal religion because it embraces all others. "
>
> SRI AUROBINDO
> HINDU SAGE

༈༈༈༈

> " The ego is like a stick dividing water into two. It creates the impression that you are one and I am another. When the ego vanishes you will realize that Brahman is your own inner Consciousness. "
>
> RAMAKRISHNA
> HINDU SAGE

HINDUS CELEBRATE KRISHNA'S BIRTH AT THE JANMASHTAMI FESTIVAL IN BOMBAY

Ancient Paganism

*A*NCIENT PAGANISM HAS *been regarded as a dead tradition since it was violently suppressed by the Christian Church of Rome in the 4th century. In recent years, however, there has been renewed interest in the spirituality of our ancestors. This Neo-Pagan revival has concentrated mainly on the more shamanic elements of Paganism. Many people now celebrate old Pagan festivals that mark the transitions of the year and honor the ancient Earth goddess, the "Green Man," and other nature spirits. But there was much more to Paganism than nature worship.*

A GREEN MAN

THE SCHOOL OF ATHENS, BY RAPHAEL

SOPHISTICATED PHILOSOPHY

The name "Pagan" means "country-dweller" and was originally a term of abuse used by early Christians to suggest that the old religion was no more than rural superstition. Actually Paganism was the sophisticated product of a high culture that laid the foundations for much of what is best in our own society.

THE MIND OF GOD

Alongside the worship of the gods and goddesses, ancient Paganism also taught the perennial spiritual philosophy of Oneness. Although the world seems to comprise many distinct things, actually all is One. This ultimate Unity is beyond the power of the intellect to comprehend, but it can be experienced directly. Plotinus explains:

"It is because the One transcends all descriptions that you can form no conception of it, yet it is always present to those with strength to touch it."

KNOW THY SELF

Above the ancient Greek sanctuary to Apollo at Delphi were inscribed the words "Know Thy Self." This is the essence of Paganism. The philosophers encourage us to transcend our mortal identity and find the true Self. When we do so, they teach, we will discover that our eternal and immortal essence is the One Soul of the Universe – the Mind of God.

> " There is one God, always still and at rest, who moves all things with the thoughts of his mind. "
>
> XENOPHANES
> ANCIENT PAGAN SAGE

❈❈❈❈

> " There are two sides to this tale. On the one hand the many unite to become the Oneness, and on the other hand the Oneness divides to become the many. Things continually shift between being united by love and divided by strife. "
>
> EMPEDOCLES
> ANCIENT PAGAN SAGE

THE EARTH MOTHER,
PAINTED BY EDWARD BURNE-JONES

LOVERS OF WISDOM

Many people have a picture of the Pagan philosophers, such as Pythagoras, Empedocles, Socrates, and Plato, as rather dry intellectuals. In fact, nothing could be further from the truth. The ancient philosophers are comparable to modern Hindu gurus. Pythagoras is generally remembered as an early mathematician, yet actually he was also a charismatic sage who dressed in flowing white robes and wore a golden coronet on his head. He was believed to have performed countless miracles, including reviving the dead, and was proclaimed a "god" by his many devotees. He is said to have known all of his own past lives and those of his followers, and claimed to be able to hear the essential harmony of the cosmos, which he called "the music of the spheres." He was the first person to call himself a "philosopher" or "lover of Wisdom."

Judaism

JUDAISM HAS PLAYED *a highly influential role in world spirituality because its monotheism has been adopted by Christianity and Islam. Its most important scripture is the Tanach. This is known to most Westerners as the Old Testament of the Christian Bible, but this name is foreign to Judaism, suggesting as it does a "New Testament" to follow it. Judaism is practiced mainly by Jews as their national religion. However, a strand of mystical Judaism, known as Cabala, has become a spiritual path for many non-Jewish people.*

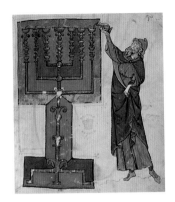

SACRED FLAMES

A RABBI READS FROM THE TORAH, A DIVISION OF THE TANACH

CABALA

Cabala is an ancient tradition that flowered in the Middle Ages. "Cabala" simply means "tradition," but it is commonly used to refer to a metaphysical diagram known also as "The Tree of Life." This is a map of consciousness, consisting of circles arranged in three columns, representing different states of being and the paths between them. It is a mystical ladder that the seeker progressively climbs toward knowledge of God.

HASIDISM

Eccentric Jewish mystics known as the "Hasids" or "Devotees" practiced a more celebratory form of Jewish spirituality that also continues to inspire many spiritual seekers. Their founder, Baal Shem, lived in 18th-century Poland. He was regarded as a heretic by orthodox Jews because he taught that what matters is devotion to God, not learning the minutiae of the Holy Law. Baal Shem expressed his love of God in dance and song rather than philosophy and learning. He once placed a highly respected book on Cabala unread on the altar, saying that although he did not understand it he was sure it was full of the most sublime wisdom. He then began to dance ecstatically around it. His dying words were "Now I know why I was created."

THE TREE OF LIFE

The outer pillars of the Tree of Life represent the fundamental polarity of the universe, often seen as male and female. The middle pillar represents the different levels of our identity. Malkut, the bottom circle, symbolizes the body self. Yesod, the second circle, represents the personality. Tiferet, the third circle, represents the Higher Self. Next comes Daat, which means knowledge. Daat represents the sublime moment in spiritual awakening when we realize that we have no independent existence apart from God. Daat is known as the "void" or the "emptiness", and so is often not portrayed on the Tree. In this state we understand the world as a Oneness "empty" of all separate things. Beyond Daat lies Keter, representing our essential being – our sense of "I am." When this is experienced in itself, no longer identified with the body or personality, it is known to be the omnipresent Consciousness of the Universe present at the heart of everyone.

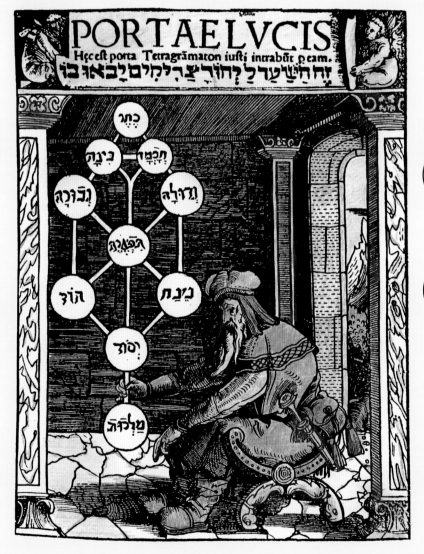

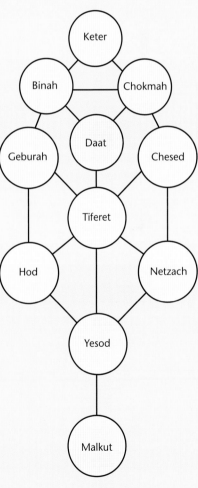

MEDIEVAL JEWISH MYSTICS DEVISED MANY DIFFERENT VERSIONS OF THE TREE OF LIFE

Christianity

CHRISTIANITY BEGAN AS *a minor group of Jewish mystics, but has become the most influential religion of all time. Fundamentalist Christians claim that Jesus Christ is the one and only Son of God and that only those who acknowledge his historical death and resurrection can be saved. Despite this tendency toward exclusivity and division, Christianity has also given rise to many great saints and sages who have taught the perennial spiritual philosophy of Unity. Today many are seeking to rediscover the mystical essence of Christianity, which, throughout its history, the religious authorities have persistently attempted to suppress.*

CHRIST WASHING FEET
OF THE DISCIPLES

EASTERN CHRISTIAN MYSTICISM

While from the earliest of times the Roman Church has emphasized dogma and blind faith, the Eastern Church, based in Constantinople, practiced a more spiritual form of Christianity. Eastern Christian mystics taught that knowing God requires us to abandon all dogma completely. Gregory of Nyssa affirms, "Every concept grasped by the mind becomes an obstacle in the quest to those who search." Whereas Western theologians thought that it was heretical for all but Jesus to believe themselves one with God, Eastern Christian sages, such as Maximus the Confessor, taught, "The whole man should become wholly God."

THE GNOSTICS

Earlier than both the Church of Rome and the Eastern Church were the Gnostic Christians. The Gnostics claimed to be the bearers of a secret mystical wisdom that imparted "Gnosis" or "Knowledge." This was not intellectual learning, but intuitive insight into the nature of God and Reality. The Gnostics did not just seek to be good Christians, they also aspired to transcend completely the personal self and become a Christ. Although these free-thinking mystics were branded heretics by Rome and brutally persecuted out of existence, the early Christian Gnostic tradition has resurfaced continually throughout history in groups such as the Cathars and the Brothers and Sisters of the Free Spirit. One anonymous Free Spirit explains their spiritual Christian teachings:

"The Spirit of Freedom is attained when one is wholly transformed into God. This union is so complete that neither the Virgin Mary nor the angels are able to distinguish between man and God. In it one is restored to one's original state, before one flowed out of Deity."

UNITED IN
PRAYER

A WINGED CHRIST ON A VENETIAN ALTAR PANEL

Abandon the Search for God

The Gnostic master Monoimos instructed his disciples in the perennial spiritual search for the source of Consciousness. He taught:

66 Abandon the search for God. Look for Him by taking yourself as the starting point. Learn who it is within you who makes everything his own and says, 'My God, my mind, my thought, my soul, my body.' Learn the source of sorrow, joy, love, hate. If you carefully investigate these matters, you will find God in your Self. 99

66 The mystery of God hugs you in its all-encompassing arms. 99

HILDEGARD DE BINGEN
CHRISTIAN MYSTIC

❄❄❄❄

66 God is nearer to me than I am to myself. 99

MEISTER ECKHART
CHRISTIAN SAGE

Islam

ISLAM WAS BORN *out of the mystical revelations of its founder the 7th-century prophet Muhammad. He received revelations from the angel Gabriel, which became the Koran – the Holy Scripture that is the foundation of Islam. "Islam" means "surrender." At its heart is the spiritual teaching of abandoning the self and its personal will, and surrendering to the divine will of God. Although recent decades have seen an upsurge of Islamic fundamentalism, which has alienated many people from Islam, many modern spiritual seekers have embraced the ecstatic path of the great Islamic mystics known as Sufism.*

A SUFI SAGE

THE SUFIS

The Sufis were regarded as dangerous heretics by fundamentalist Muslims, and some, such as Al Hallaj, were executed by the Islamic authorities. While fundamentalists have interpreted Muhammad's concept of the "Jihad" or "Holy War" as a call to wage bloody crusades to enforce conversion to Islam, the Sufis thought of the "Jihad" as an internal battle to overcome the self and surrender to God. They taught that it is only the illusion of being an individual self, separate from God, that veils God from us. Our normal state of awareness, in which we experience ourselves as a separate person, is a type of sleep from which we must awaken. When we do, we will see that God is everywhere, everyone, and everything.

MUSLIM GIRLS PREPARE FOR WORSHIP

No Room for "Me"

A man knocked on God's door. "Who's there?" asked God from within. "It's me," said the man. "Go away then. There's no room here for two," said God. The man departed and wandered in the arid desert until he realized his error. Returning to the door, he knocked once again. "Who's there?" asked God, as before. "You," answered the man. "Then come in," God replied.

SUFI TEACHING STORY

SACRED LOVE POETRY

Many of the great Sufis wrote inspired spiritual poetry. To express the intensity of their longing for God and the ecstasy of mystical communion, the Sufis often turned to images of intoxication and romantic love. For the Sufis, God is an intimate "Beloved" with whom they share a passionate, sacred love affair.

I drank You down in one,
collapsing intoxicated by purity.
Ever since, I can't tell if I exist or not.
Sometimes I know the bliss
of the "I" that looks through my eyes.
Other times my habits dump me back in the shit.
But then there it is – that aroma once again.
I'm returned to the Rose Garden.

JALAL AL-DIN RUMI
SUFI SAGE

My heart brimming with Your hope
*   is the rarest of riches.*
My tongue tasting Your Name is the
*   sweetest of flavors.*
Moments passed with You transcend time.
Yet I remain a lonesome stranger in Your world.
This is why I am complaining.

RABI'A
SUFI POETESS

66 When you seek Him, look for Him in your looking.
    Closer to you than yourself to yourself. 99

JALAL AL-DIN RUMI

※※※

66 Love is to stand before your Beloved,
    Stripped naked of all attributes,
So that His qualities become your qualities. 99

AL-HALLAJ
SUFI SAINT

A BLACK STONE, BELIEVED TO ABSORB THE SINS OF PILGRIMS WHO TOUCH IT, IS BUILT INTO A SHRINE AT MECCA

Taoism

TAO

TAOISM IS A CHINESE SPIRITUAL PHILOSOPHY that has become popular through the spread of martial arts, which it inspired, such as Tai Chi Chuan and Aikido. The Tao Te Ching, an enigmatic spiritual masterpiece attributed to the Taoist sage Lao Tzu, is a constant source of inspiration to many modern seekers. "Tao" is Chinese for "way". Tao is "the way it is," "the way life works," the natural unfolding of existence. Tao is the fundamental Nature of Reality, the underlying Oneness, the great Ocean of Being, the Primal Source.

THE WAY OF WATER

Taoism is about learning to live in harmony with Tao by abandoning the futile attempt to control the tides of perpetual transformation and instead to go with the flow of life. Taoism is known as the "Way of Water" because Taoists seek to embody the yielding qualities of water. Like water, which flows around any obstacle it confronts, they seek to accommodate rather than confront problems. Like water, which is soft and weak yet has the power to wear away hard rocks, they trust in the strength of acceptance and perseverance rather than effort and force. Like a river rushing to the ocean, Taoists seek to transform their lives into a journey back to Tao.

WU WEI – NO DOER

A central practice of Taoism is the cultivation of the state of "wu wei." This phrase is often translated as "not doing," but the Taoist sages are not encouraging us to do nothing. This is obviously an impossibility for a human being. They want us to recognize that there is in reality "no doer." All that we do and think and feel is an expression of Tao through a particular

MASTER PERFORMING TAI CHI CHUAN

body and mind. To live truly in harmony with Tao is to be in the state of "wu wei" in which we have no sense of being a separate individual to interfere with the natural organic unfolding of existence.

YIN AND YANG

Taoism teaches that everything in life has its complementary pole – day and night, male and female, seer and seen, subject and object, yes and no, pleasure and pain, quality and quantity, life and death. Taoists call this omnipresent polarity that underlies all of life "Yin" and "Yang." The constant flux we call reality is created by the process of Yin and Yang perpetually changing into each other. This fundamental rhythm of life is symbolically represented by the familiar Yin\Yang symbol in which the dark Yin segment is shown with a white spot of Yang, and vice versa. Yin and Yang are united in the circle of Tao. Although Yin and Yang are opposites, they are also complementaries that can only exist together. They are like two ends of one piece of string. They are the dual expressions of the paradoxical Oneness of Tao.

66 Just surrender to the wave
of the Great Change.
Neither happy nor afraid.
And when it is time to go,
then simply go –
without any unnecessary fuss. 99

T'AO CH'IEN
TAOIST SAGE

❧❧❧

66 The wise know
there is no one
to go anywhere.
There is seeing,
but no one looking.
Doing naturally arises
from Being. 99

LAO TZU
TAOIST SAGE

THE YIN AND THE YANG

Buddhism

SINCE THE CHINESE occupation of Tibet, many Tibetan Buddhist teachers have taken refuge in the West, attracting a large number of modern seekers to Buddhism. Buddhism was inspired by an Indian sage named Siddhartha Guatama (b. 560 BCE), more commonly known by the title of "Buddha." He was not concerned with metaphysical speculation, but with guiding his students toward the experience of enlightenment. The Tibetan word for Buddhist is "nangpa," which means "insider." Buddhism is about looking inside to discover the essential nature of the mind.

BUDDHA

SAMSARA

Buddhism teaches that our lives are full of suffering because we mistakenly believe ourselves to be a body that is born to die. But in reality there is no separate "self" at all. In fact, there are no separate individual entities, because all things are so intimately interrelated that nothing has any independent existence. The world of separate things is an illusion, which Buddhists call "samsara," and the idea of ourselves as separate beings is part of that illusion.

NIRVANA

Enlightenment is the experience of "nirvana" – the "extinguishing" of the illusion of the self. This is a blissful state of being pure Consciousness. This is our true identity or Buddha-Nature. We are the Mind of the Universe. Yet Buddhism does not reject the illusionary world of appearances. It teaches that, since all is One, "samsara is nirvana and nirvana is samsara." The world is an appearance in Consciousness, but Consciousness is only experienced because of the appearances.

STATUE OF A TIBETAN BUDDHIST DEITY

A DROP OF WATER RETURNING TO THE OCEAN

The experience of abandoning the illusion of being an individual self is often compared to a drop of water dissolving back into the mighty ocean. This metaphor can seem to imply that we are going to be annihilated, which does not sound particularly appealing. But this is a complete misunderstanding. Buddhism teaches that the separate self cannot cease to be because it never existed. It was merely a transitory illusion. The enlightened are not lost in the overwhelming vastness of the Ocean of Being. They know that there has only ever been the Ocean. The separate self is like a wave upon the sea that, although apparently distinct, is actually no more than a disturbance on the surface of the water. Relinquishing the illusion of separateness is not annihilation. It is the knowledge that our essential being cannot possibly die. When the wave crashes onto the shore, the ocean is not diminished, and we are that ocean. This was why when the Buddha was asked if a person who attains enlightenment could be said to still exist, he enigmatically replied, "It would be wrong to say he does and it would be wrong to say he doesn't."

It is your own awareness right now.
It is simple, natural, and clear.
Why say "I don't understand what the mind is"?
There is nothing to think about,
just permanent clear Consciousness.
Why say "I don't see the reality of the mind"?
The mind is the thinker of these thoughts.
Why say "When I look I can't find it"?
No looking is necessary.
Why say "Whatever I try doesn't work"?
It is enough to remain simple.
Why say "I can't achieve this"?
The void of pure Consciousness is naturally present.

PADMA SAMBHAVA
BUDDHIST SAGE

❝ Buddhism is a clever way to enjoy life. ❞

THICH NHAT HANH
BUDDHIST SAGE

❧❧❧❧

❝ Know emptiness. Be compassionate. ❞

MILAREPA
BUDDHIST SAGE

BUDDHIST MONKS IN THAILAND CARRY BOWLS TO RECEIVE OFFERINGS OF FOOD

Zen

Z EN IS A *synthesis of Indian Buddhism and Chinese Taoism. Its founder was an Indian Buddhist named "Bodhidharma" or "Knower of the Way." In the 6th century CE he journeyed from India to China where he founded a school of Buddhism known as "Ch'an," which in 12th-century Japan acquired the familiar name "Zen." Zen is a vibrant and anarchic approach to spirituality, which emphasizes direct experience and irreverence toward religious formalities. This has led to it being enthusiastically embraced by many modern seekers, often outside a specifically Buddhist context.*

BODHIDHARMA

SEEING ONE'S OWN NATURE IS BUDDHAHOOD

Zen is not an organized set of teachings. It is about discovering who we are. Master Bassui reduced Zen teachings to one phrase: "Seeing one's own nature is Buddhahood." Zen is not a philosophy. Zen is about emptying the mind of thoughts and experiencing the mind itself. The empty mind is our true Buddha-Nature. In the emptiness of pure Consciousness there is no sense of being a separate individual, but rather of being One with all that is.

GET REAL!

Zen wants us to "get real!", not to be lost in abstract metaphysical speculations. When a student substitutes an understanding of Zen philosophy for the experience of enlightenment toward which it points, the Zen masters are compassionately merciless in bringing the student down to earth. There is a story of a young student who visited master Dokuon hoping to show off his understanding of Zen. In an erudite manner he proudly expounded Buddhist teachings for some time, eventually concluding, "In reality nothing exists." Master Dokuon sat silently smoking, ignoring the pupil who became increasingly agitated. Suddenly Dokuon whacked him with his bamboo pipe, making him yell with anger. "If nothing exists," inquired the master with a smile, "where did this anger come from?"

BLACK-ROBED ZEN MONKS

ZANY ZEN MASTERS

Zen masters are renowned for acting in bizarre and seemingly illogical ways to get their teachings across. There is a famous story of a professor who once visited a master to learn about Zen. While serving him tea the master kept on pouring after the cup was full, spilling tea everywhere. The professor was horrified, exclaiming "Stop! Stop!" The master smiled and said, "The cup is full and can take no more tea. In the same way, your mind is full of ideas. To learn Zen, you must empty it."

Enter the Moment

Zen teaches us to dissolve our sense of being an individual separate from the rest of life into the immediacy of the present moment. When we are fully in the here and now, there is only the unfolding flux of life being witnessed by Consciousness, without any sense of separation. When a student asked to be shown the way to enlightenment, his master replied, "Do you hear that babbling brook? Enter there."

❝ Find the silence that contains thoughts. ❞

HAKUIN
ZEN MASTER

❧❧❧❧

❝ Our Buddha-Nature is there from the beginning,
like the sun obscured by clouds. ❞

HO-SHAN
ZEN MASTER

The way of the artist

POETRY, PAINTING, AND MUSIC *are not religious traditions. But being a creative artist can be a spiritual path that requires an imaginative leap into the unknown; a dive into the great sea of mystery; a stirring up of that deep mind that can sing the Song of Life and so communicate with others across all personal boundaries. For many people, being a creative artist is a way of exploring spirituality without having to be religious.*

W. B. YEATS

POETS

Poetry originated in sacred songs of praise to charm the gods and goddesses and has always been an expression of spirituality. Many mystics from all traditions – the Hindu saint Kabir, the Christian mystic St. John of the Cross, the Islamic Sufi Jalal al-Din Rumi, and the outrageous Zen master Ikkyu to name a few – were also exquisite poets able to express their struggles and ecstasies with poignant beauty. Some mystical poets have not been part of any religious tradition, such as Walt Whitman who spontaneously discovered for himself the perennial spiritual philosophy that informs his work. Other great mystical poets of the Western world include William Wordsworth, whose spirituality was rooted in communing with Nature; W. B. Yeats, who was a member of the Occult fraternity of the Golden Dawn; Robert Graves, who became a modern devotee of Isis, the White Goddess of the ancient Egyptians; and T. S. Eliot, whose sublime poems "The Four Quartets" are testimonies to his deep understanding of the world's mystical traditions.

ROMAN ACTOR AS BUCCO, THE BRAGGING COMIC FIGURE OF ANCIENT ROMAN COMEDY

ARTISTS

Painting and sculpture were also originally sacred pursuits. In ancient times, artists represented the forms of the gods and goddesses as a focus for devotion. Renaissance painters, such as the great sage Leonardo da Vinci, were members of a revived Academy modeled on Plato's original brotherhood of mystics, which maintained this tradition. Botticelli painted his famous picture of the Pagan goddess Venus at a precise astrological moment to be a talisman of occult radiance. Modern artists, too, have seen their work as inherently spiritual. Kandinski was immersed in Theosophy. He attributed spiritually symbolic meanings to colors and forms. Blue, for example, he regarded as the most divine of all colors.

THEATER AND MUSIC

Theater also has its roots in spirituality. It developed from ancient Pagan rites that dramatized the myths of the gods. Many great playwrights, such as Euripides, Shakespeare, and Goethe, were also mystics and philosophers. Music, too, has been an integral part of spirituality since the primal peoples called the spirits with their primitive drums and didgeridoos. In the sophisticated Pagan Mystery religion of the Pythagoreans, music became a sacred science through which one could experience the "Music of the Spheres" – the primal harmony of the Universe. Those people, such as Mozart and Beethoven, who are

Van Morrison

reach beyond their normal awareness into the mysterious world of the imagination, we find the recognition of life as a spiritual journey. Artists, poets, and musicians, often the very worst sorts of people by the standards of conventional morality, have been some of the greatest explorers of spirituality who have returned from their adventures to create the richest of human culture. Their spirituality is often intensely individualistic and libertarian, in reaction to the proscriptive and prescriptive nature of organized religion.

BEAUTY

The Way of the Artist is above all about the spiritual power of Beauty. The Pagan mystical philosopher Plato described God as "the Good, the Beautiful, and the True." The artist is not concerned with Truth like the philosopher or Goodness like the saint. The Way of the Artist is a celebration of Beauty – not as something to be analyzed and understood but as an awe-inspiring mystery on which to become intoxicated.

able to plumb the depths of the imagination and hear these hidden harmonies, have brought us back testimonies to the awesome beauty of creation, which evoke exquisite spiritual states of awareness.

SOUL MUSIC

Modern musicians still seek to spiritually inspire their audiences. The Beatles proclaimed the perennial message of the mystics: "All You Need is Love." The funk band Earth Wind and Fire rapped about "mysticism" and covered their album sleeves with ancient Egyptian spiritual symbols. The pop band The Police proclaimed through radios across the planet, "We are spirits in a material world." The rhythm and blues singer Van Morrison sings songs with titles such as *Enlightenment*, including lyrics about Socrates and T. S. Eliot.

THE MYSTERIES OF IMAGINATION

The truth is that spirituality is not the preserve of the religiously inclined or the fanatically moral. Wherever human beings

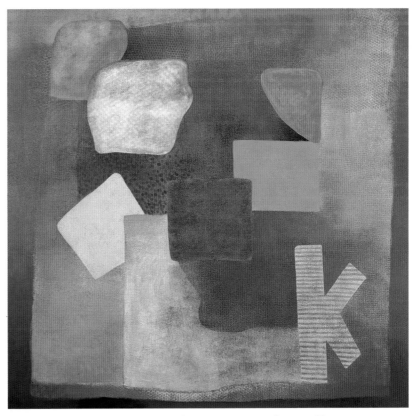

From the Hitchcock Series, *painted by Robert Natkin*

SPIRITUAL POETRY

WILLIAM BLAKE

The epitaph of the poet and painter William Blake remembers him also as a "mystic." He writes that "Painting as well as music and poetry exists and exults in immortal thoughts." He describes himself as "a God-intoxicated man" who is "drunk with intellectual vision." This spiritual inebriation does not distort reality, but reveals it. Blake explains that when "the doors of perception" are cleansed "everything appears as it is, infinite."

Auguries of Innocence

To see a world in a Grain of Sand
And a Heaven in a Wild Flower,
Hold Infinity in the palm of your hand
And Eternity in an hour.

WILLIAM BLAKE

The Garden of Love

I went to the Garden of Love,
And saw what I never had seen;
A chapel was built in the midst,
Where I used to play on the green.

And the gates of the Chapel were shut,
And "Thou shalt not" writ over the door;
So I turn'd to the Garden of Love
That so many sweet flowers bore;

And I saw it was filled with graves,
And tomb-stones where the flowers should be;
And Priests in black gowns were walking their rounds,
And binding with briars my joy and desires.

WILLIAM BLAKE

"WHEN THE MORNING STARS SANG TOGETHER,"
PAINTED BY WILLIAM BLAKE

WALT WHITMAN

The 19th-century poet Walt Whitman wrote poems of passionate wonder and mystical insight. He was not a member of any religion, but a natural sage. His friend, Dr Bucke, writes of him, "Perhaps, indeed, no man ever lived who liked so many things and disliked so few as Walt Whitman. When I first knew him, I used to think that he watched himself, and would not allow his tongue to give expression to fretfulness, antipathy, complaint, and remonstrance. It did not occur to me as possible that these mental states could be absent in him. After long observation, however, I am satisfied that such absence or unconsciousness was entirely real. He never spoke deprecatingly of any nationality or class of men, or time in the world's history, or against any trades or occupations – not even against any animals, insects, or inanimate things, not any of the laws of nature, nor any of the results of those laws, such as illness, deformity, and death. He never swore. He could not very well, since he never spoke in anger and apparently never was angry. He never exhibited fear, and I do not believe he ever felt it."

The Spirit

Santa Spirita, breather, life,
Beyond the light, lighter than light,
Beyond the flames of hell – joyous,
  leaping easily above hell;
Beyond Paradise – perfumed solely
  with mine own perfume;
Including all life on earth – touching, including
  God – including Savior and Satan;
Ethereal, pervading all – for, without me,
  what were all? what were God?
Essence of forms – life of the real identities,
  permanent, positive, namely the unseen,
Life of the great round world, the sun and stars,
  and of man – I, the General Soul.

WALT WHITMAN

" The road of excess leads to the palace of wisdom. "

WILLIAM BLAKE

❧❧❧❧

" Eternity is in love with the productions of time. "

WILLIAM BLAKE

❧❧❧❧

" Mysteries are like the sun,
dazzling, yet plain to all eyes. "

JOHN DONNE

❧❧❧❧

" Beauty is truth, truth beauty –
that is all ye know on earth,
and all ye need to know. "

JOHN KEATS

JOHN KEATS

Natural spirituality

SPIRITUAL EXPERIENCES ARE natural. Any event can suddenly trigger spontaneous illumination. The dizzy heights of romantic love. The agony of tragic death. The ecstasy of sex. A shaft of sunlight through some trees. The familiar affection of family life. The harsh camaraderie of war. The concentrated passion of competitive sports. The culture shock of foreign travel. A kind word from a stranger. We do not have to follow a spiritual tradition to explore spirituality. All of life is an opportunity to awaken.

THE BEAUTY OF NATURE

Many people who regard themselves as "unreligious" experience spiritual states through being overcome by the beauty of Nature. Although regarded as an atheist, the 19th-century writer Richard Jefferies' love of Nature inspired the same spiritual insights as the great saints of the world's religions. He writes in rapture of recognizing his "own inner consciousness" so clearly that his awareness moved beyond time to a place where he was one with whatever he witnessed in a perfect and eternal now.

SPIRITUAL SCIENCE

Science is the study of Nature. Although today it is widely regarded as the great opponent of spirituality, for many it has actually been a source of spiritual inspiration. The founding fathers of science, such as Pythagoras and Archimedes, were initiates of the Pagan Mystery religion who believed that through discovering the beautiful order of the cosmos one would oneself become beautifully ordered. This mystical vision of science inspired many of the great scientists who have shaped our modern understanding of the world. Newton's work on physics defined the scientific world view until the 20th century, yet he saw his mystical treatise on alchemy and astrology as of far greater significance than his far less numerous scientific writings. The next great scientific revolutionary, Albert Einstein, saw himself as investigating "God's thoughts." One of the founders of quantum physics, Niels Bohr, put the Taoist Yin/Yang symbol on his coat of arms.

THE GREAT SMOKY MOUNTAINS, CALIFORNIA

66 Realizing that spirit, recognizing my own inner consciousness, the psyche so clearly, I cannot understand time. Now is eternity; now is the immortal life. Here this moment, by this hill, on earth, now; I exist in it. 99

RICHARD JEFFERIES

ALBERT EINSTEIN

With his wild hair and otherworldly eccentricities, Albert Einstein has become a modern archetype of the inspired scientist and sage, capable of seeing beyond the physical world to the underlying reality. Einstein was working as a watchmaker when he came up with his Theory of Relativity, which revolutionized physics. He writes of his experience of science in words that could be those of the great mystics:

66 The most important function of science is to awaken the cosmic religious feeling and keep it alive. It is very difficult to explain this feeling to anyone who is entirely without it. The individual feels the nothingness of human desires and aims, and the sublimity and marvelous order that reveal themselves both in nature and in the world of thought. He looks upon individual existence as a sort of prison and wants to experience the universe as a single significant whole. 99

66 The most beautiful thing we can experience is the mysterious. It is the source of all true art and all science. He to whom this emotion is a stranger, who can no longer pause to wonder and stand rapt in awe, is as good as dead: his eyes are closed. 99

New spiritual traditions

THE LAST FEW DECADES *have seen the birth of many new spiritual movements. They are often dismissed as "cults" by the mainstream religions who accuse their leaders of brainwashing the gullible and breaking up families. This is a little ironic however, because nearly all the founders of the mainstream religions were accused of being dangerous fanatics, and both Buddha and Jesus, for example, are said to have encouraged their adherents to abandon their families. Is this modern paranoia about cults any more than the big old cults feeling threatened by the little new cults?*

SUN MYUNG MOON

MESSIAHS OR MERCENARIES

Some modern spiritual movements offer new forms of spirituality, such as the Church of Scientology set up by L. Ron Hubbard, which draws on elements of popular psychology, occultism, and science fantasy. Other new spiritual movements are imports of traditional Eastern spirituality to the West, such as the Maharishi's Transcendental Meditation movement made famous by the Beatles. Some are a new combination of traditional elements taken from various sources, such as The Unification Church, better known as the Moonies. This cult was set up by the Korean Reverend Sun Myung Moon. He teaches a combination of Christianity and traditional Korean spirituality, and claims to be the returning Christ.

WHO CAN SAY?

To their followers, the leaders of all these movements are divine saviors, but outsiders routinely portray them as money-making mercenaries. Some of these powerfully charismatic individuals may indeed be wise and compassionate sages; often, however, they are obviously dangerous egomaniacs. This has certainly been the case in recent years with a number of pseudo-gurus, such as the Reverend Jim Jones, who have led their followers in tragic mass suicides. Except for such extreme cases, however, it is almost impossible to judge the merits or otherwise of new spiritual movements from the outside, because the fear and misunderstanding they generate give

THE MASS WEDDING OF 30,000 MOONIES IN 1997

them so much bad press that an extremely distorted picture is created. Unfortunately, it can also be very difficult to judge a spiritual movement from the inside, because members can easily become sucked into the cult's picture of the world, in which doubting the dogmas of the group is unthinkable.

THE SPIRITUAL DANGERS OF RELIGION

Many people who have become involved with new cults have ultimately come away feeling that they have been let down or even psychologically damaged. But people have always been damaged by religion, whether they be fundamentalist Catholics who have been brought up to

feel guilty of original sin or fundamentalist Hindus who have been brought up to believe themselves to be born in a low caste because of bad actions in previous lives. Becoming a member of any spiritual group is fraught with dangers and requires us to use all the powers of our discriminating mind and intuitive heart. Thankfully, most people who get involved with one of the new religions (or one of the old ones!) come through the experience wiser for it – either because they have learned from a genuine teacher or because they have lost their naivete and learned to discriminate between real spirituality and a flashy front. Being disappointed by false teachers is often part of the process of becoming spiritually mature.

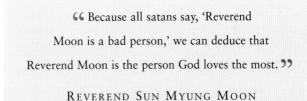

66 Because all satans say, 'Reverend Moon is a bad person,' we can deduce that Reverend Moon is the person God loves the most. 99

REVEREND SUN MYUNG MOON
FOUNDER OF THE UNIFICATION CHURCH

❊❊❊❊

66 I'd like to start a religion. That's where the money is. 99

L. RON HUBBARD
SCIENCE FICTION WRITER
AND FOUNDER OF SCIENTOLOGY

A JEHOVAH'S WITNESS SPEAKS AT A MEETING

Scientology

Scientology is a modern cult currently very popular among the "glitterati" of Hollywood. It was set up by the science fiction writer L. Ron Hubbard who wrote a bestseller called *Dianetics,* which claimed to be a science of the mind capable of helping people achieve their full potential. Hubbard taught that, through contacting and reliving painful memories by using a combination of counseling and a sort of lie detector, it was possible to become a "Clear" – a perfect individual. Later he set up the Church of Scientology and incorporated various spiritual ideas, teaching that we each have a "thetan," an immortal soul, which his techniques could help us discover.

Intimate friends and close associates have constantly questioned Hubbard's integrity, suggesting that he began his movement as a cynical moneymaking venture and an attempt at self-aggrandizement. Whether this is true or not, by the end of his life he had certainly convinced himself as well as his followers that he was the most important person ever to have lived – the savior of humankind who was being persecuted by a hostile world. Although he was extremely charismatic and loved attention during his early years, he died in hiding, unkempt and consumed by strange fears and paranoias. To his followers, however, he had merely gone on to research "the next level."

FOLLOWERS OF INDIAN GURU BHAGWAN SHREE RAJNEESH, WHO BELIEVE IN SPIRITUAL AND SEXUAL FREEDOM

MAHARAJI

Many Indian gurus have come to the West and set up new spiritual movements. One of the most extraordinary is known to his followers by the common Indian title "Maharaji." There can be no doubt that Maharaji is a remarkable individual. Born the youngest son of an established Indian guru, Maharaji was a child prodigy. He practiced meditation when little more than an infant and, at the age of eight, when his father died, announced himself to be the new "Perfect Master" who would bring peace to the world. He soon found himself with a following of millions. Aged just 13, he came to the West where he was adored and ridiculed as the "Boy Guru."

Originally his organization, known then as the Divine Light Mission, was an exotic Hindu cult that hailed the young guru as God incarnate. Since this time, however, he has completely dumped all the Hindu trappings that he grew up with and now presents a form of spirituality that is decidedly unreligious, teaches no dogmas, and emphasizes personal experience through practicing the simple meditation techniques he calls "Knowledge." He now lives in California but constantly travels the world in his own jet, which he pilots himself, addressing his many followers. His affluent lifestyle has attracted much criticism, but Maharaji's message is one of enjoying the gift of life, not religious austerity.

MAHARAJI AGED 15 YEARS

66 I have not come to establish a new religion or sect, but I have come to give you Knowledge of Truth. If you come to me with a guileless heart you will surely receive this most ancient spiritual Knowledge, which if practiced upon, will give us perfect peace of mind. 99

MAHARAJI
AGED 13 YEARS

Psychedelic drugs

IN RECENT YEARS *many people have used psychedelic drugs to explore altered states of awareness outside the context of a religious tradition. Although mainstream society associates drugs with criminals and losers, this movement was inspired by doctors of psychology and eminent intellectuals. They discovered the "psychedelic" or "consciousness-expanding" properties of plants traditionally used by indigenous shamans. Later they pioneered research into synthesized psychedelics, such as LSD, which led to an explosion of interest in spirituality and inspired the 1960's spirit of peace and love.*

"BED-IN" FOR PEACE

EXPLORERS OF CONSCIOUSNESS

The author Aldous Huxley, who had a comprehensive knowledge of world spirituality, believed the LSD experience was comparable to the spiritual experiences of the saints and sages, and even took LSD on his deathbed. Alan Watts, who played an important role in bringing Eastern spirituality to the West, was initially skeptical of the spiritual value of LSD – that is until he experienced it for himself! He writes of experiencing the perennial spiritual revelation of an intelligent love permeating the universe. The psychedelic experiences of Dr. Richard Alpert, who pioneered LSD research with Dr. Timothy Leary at Harvard University, initiated a lifelong exploration of spirituality, during which time he has become a respected spiritual teacher better known today as "Ram Dass."

ALDOUS HUXLEY

A THREAT TO SOCIETY

Mainstream society feels psychedelics threaten its very foundation and has relentlessly persecuted those who use them. Leary and Alpert were hounded out of Harvard, and Leary was later imprisoned. Psychedelic drugs were made illegal and users were labeled as depraved or stupid. Despite this, the allure of easy access to altered states has proved too great, and drug use has mushroomed. Millions of people have now directly experienced drug-induced mystical experiences, which has initiated a cultural revolution that is still underway.

DRUG USE AND ABUSE

Drug abuse can be dangerous. But there is no doubt that some drugs, especially when taken in the right context and with the right intention, can induce powerfully transformative spiritual experiences. To deny either of these facts is to oversimplify the dilemma modern society faces with drug use and abuse. However, recreational drug use is often a form of escapism, whereas shamanic power plants are traditionally used to gain entrance to what is known to be a potentially dangerous spiritual dimension. Users of shamanic drugs are purified through ritual, supervised by those more experienced, and undertake the experience in a sacred context. None of this is available for the vast majority of those using psychedelics today, which can lead to confusion and drug abuse.

MODERN-DAY TRIBAL DANCING – A TRANSFORMATIVE EXPERIENCE

ECSTASY

Despite this, however, even among recreational users a huge number of people do spontaneously enter altered states of awareness and have their view of reality significantly transformed. Are psychedelics a modern form of power plant Shamanism? It is hard to ignore the obvious comparison between ancient indigenous rites and the spectacle of tribes of young people dancing wildly from dusk to dawn to an insistent beat under the transformative power of the appropriately named "Ecstasy." It is a reflection of our culture's fear of ecstatic states and obsession with sterile safety that the spiritual power of psychedelic drugs is rarely even mentioned in the drugs debate. Meanwhile those whose spiritual explorations include using psychedelics find themselves branded as criminals.

> " My Soul became aware of God.
> I felt him streaming in like light upon me.
> I cannot describe the ecstasy I felt. "
>
> J.A. SYMONDS
> VICTORIAN EXPLORER OF PSYCHEDELICS

> " I felt as if I were out of my body.
> I thought I had died. "
>
> ALBERT HOFMANN
> CREATOR OF LSD

The New Age movement

THE *"HOLISTIC" OR "New Age" movement is a diverse collection of small groups who share not so much one creed as an attitude of optimistic faith in the future, a belief in personal growth, and an open-mindedness toward nontraditional forms of spirituality, alternative lifestyles, and supernatural phenomena. The New Age movement is often uncritical, some might say naive or even gullible. Everything you can imagine is found somewhere in this loose alliance of eclectic visionaries.*

GAIA

OPEN-MINDED OR SIMPLE-MINDED?

Channeling of disembodied spirits, healing with crystals, worship of Gaia the Earth Goddess, every sort of divination, contacts with extraterrestrials, communicating with dolphins, alternative therapies, Eastern medicine, immortalism, past-life regression, conversing with angels, exploration of ley lines, becoming successful through using the power of the mind, even supposed genetic reprogramming, are all on offer through books and weekend workshops, which often promise miraculous transformation.

SPIRITUAL INDIVIDUALISM

The great virtue of the New Age movement is that it gives a spiritual dimension to modern individualism. It frees people from feeling they must join an established religion in order to have a spiritual life, and empowers individuals to find a set of beliefs and practices that are right for them personally. However, New Age spirituality can be superficial. Because it concentrates so much on empowering individuals to become more successful and fulfill their deepest desires, it often ignores the perennial spiritual teaching of selflessness. New Age spirituality runs the risk of encouraging adherents to become more powerful people, rather than transcending the personality altogether and discovering their deeper nature.

GODDESS WORSHIP IN CALIFORNIA

The Age of Aquarius

The New Age movement acquires its name from its preoccupation with the coming new astrological Age of Aquarius. Astronomical changes in the relationship of the stars are interpreted as meaning that the current Age of Pisces, which began about 2,000 years ago, is coming to an end. This has given rise to an optimistic vision of a new golden era of spiritual enlightenment, often accompanied by apocalyptic fears that there will first be great natural disasters and social collapse. At the time of the last change in Ages there was a similar explosion of new spiritual ideas, eclecticism, and apocalyptic visions. In the West, the Piscean age did, in fact, give birth to a new form of spirituality – the Christian religion. Like certain New Age groups today, many early Christians believed that the end of the world was imminent. The spiritual characteristics that have defined the Age of Pisces did not come to prominence overnight, however, but took many hundreds of years to develop. It seems likely, therefore, that any changes that are coming in the New Age of Aquarius will also not be widespread in the immediate future.

66 The holistic movement is in the process of reinventing, perhaps rediscovering, the nature of religion. It rejects the classic modern definition of religion as a set of particular beliefs held by a particular group and comes back to the idea that there is a natural, normal, and healthy human instinct and ability both to connect with the beauty and wonder of nature and the universe, and to explore consciousness and identity. 99

WILLIAM BLOOM
NEW AGE VISIONARY

66 When we really love ourselves everything in our life works. 99

LOUISE L. HAY
NEW AGE TEACHER

PART TWO

SPIRITUAL PRACTICES

An examination of traditional and
modern spiritual practices and
how to use them in everyday life

SPIRITUAL PRACTICES

ALL SPIRITUAL TRADITIONS *teach techniques to help seekers transform themselves and their lives. This section explores some of these traditional practices and suggests simple ways you can try them out for yourself. To take a practice to any depth it is usually best to work within the tradition with a qualified and experienced teacher. However, by experimenting with some of the practices here, you can gain a feeling for which techniques you may wish to master more fully in the future. Try out those practices to which you feel personally drawn. Trust your intuition to guide you. If you find a practice helpful, return to it often.*

*BUDDHIST MONKS SIT
IN QUIET MEDITATION*

❝ Religious people insist that to be spiritual
we should sing certain songs in prescribed ways
and live a certain lifestyle
and obey certain moral codes
and adopt certain ways of speaking
and so on and so on.

Stop! Enough!
I cannot go along with this nonsense.
To live a spiritual life
we need only be what we naturally are. ❞

CHUANG TZU
TAOIST SAGE

ABORIGINES PERFORM ELABORATE RITUALS

BE RELAXED AND ALERT

Each of these spiritual practices is unique, but there are some general guidelines that are worth remembering. Relax your body and clear your mind of any worries and anxieties that may be bothering you. If distracting thoughts arise, don't follow them but let them simply pass away. Nurture a receptive and alert state of awareness. Try not to have too many expectations. Don't try too hard, and above all be patient and kind to yourself.

PRACTICE IN A PEACEFUL PLACE

Many of these spiritual techniques can be practiced anywhere, but to begin with it is helpful to practice in a conducive environment without too many distractions. Choose a place where you feel peaceful and it is easy to concentrate – perhaps a favorite room or a natural beauty spot. Set aside a period of time when you will not be disturbed. If you are at home, don't forget to turn off the telephone!

PRACTICE REGULARLY

Spiritual techniques are about transforming our habitual states of mind and awakening a new spiritual consciousness. This usually takes time and perseverance. It is a good idea, therefore, to make your spiritual practice a regular part of daily life. Although many spiritual techniques can be practiced at any time, it is best to begin by practicing at a particular time, for example first thing in the morning or last thing at night. This will help you to make your practice consistent.

SPIRITUAL PRACTICE CAN HELP YOU FEEL MORE ALIVE

PLAY AT SPIRITUALITY

The rewards of such self-discipline can be great, but don't turn your spiritual practice into a chore that you feel you *should* perform. If you do so, you will quickly lose interest and stop practicing. Play at spirituality. It is an exciting journey into the unknown that can be full of captivating challenges and uplifting surprises. Enjoy yourself.

STAY OPEN AT ALL TIMES

These techniques are powerful ways to stimulate moments of heightened spiritual awareness in which the awesome beauty and profound depths of life are revealed. But such experiences will not necessarily occur while you are performing your spiritual practice. They can arise at any time, often when we are least expecting them, so remain as open as you can at all times. Spiritual experiences can not be forced, but always have the quality of "grace" or a gift. All we can do is be ever ready to receive.

The King and the Mango

A king asked a sage to tell him about enlightenment. The sage replied, "How would you convey the taste of a something sweet to someone who had never eaten anything sweet?" The king could find no answer and announced, "It's impossible. You tell me." The sage picked up a mango and handed it to the king saying, "This is very sweet. Try eating it!"

HINDU TEACHING STORY

Mahatma Gandhi

Whether engaged in international politics or mundane chores, Mahatma Ghandi turned everything he did into a spiritual practice. He adopted a life of voluntary austerity, even spinning his own basic clothing, and preached "Live simply so that others may simply live."

66 Seek and you will be troubled.

Be troubled and you will be astonished.

Be astonished and you will rule over all things. 99

JESUS

THE GNOSTIC GOSPEL OF THOMAS

꠸꠸꠸꠸

66 You can't always retreat from the world

to a country house, the seashore, or the

mountains. But it is always in your power

to retreat into yourself. Give yourself to

this retreat; renew and increase your

soul completely. 99

MARCUS AURELIUS

PAGAN SAGE

66 Stir like an embryo.

Evolve senses that can witness Light.

Mature in this womb-world,

and prepare for your second birth

out of earth into the limitless. 99

JALAL AL-DIN RUMI

SUFI SAGE

꠸꠸꠸꠸

66 To actively seek union with Tao

is to attempt the impossible. 99

CHUANG TZU

TAOIST SAGE

KEEP A SPIRITUAL DIARY

As you spiritually awaken, you will experience many insights that may be worth jotting down on a piece of paper. You can contemplate these personal realizations at a later date. You may like to keep a spiritual diary in which to record your thoughts and feelings each day.

A PERSONAL JOURNEY OF TRANSFORMATION

Spirituality is not about joining a club or trying to shape ourselves in imitation of some exemplary role model. It is about each one of us discovering our true Self, and we can only do this for ourselves. It is no help just to talk about transformation; we must be transformed ourselves. It is no good just studying how the saints and sages made the spiritual pilgrimage; we must have the courage to set off on the journey ourselves. Although others can guide and support us, we must find the personal resources to meet the particular challenges that lie in store for us. If we do, we are promised certain success. The Christian mystic Brother Lawrence encourages, "Knock, persevere in knocking, and I guarantee you will be answered." The Hindu guru Sai Baba assures us, "All those who walk with God reach their destination."

WRITE DOWN YOUR INSIGHTS

LIFE IS THE WAY

Spiritual techniques are not the Way; they are methods of waking up to the fact that all of life is the Way. Spiritual practices help us live more consciously and so enable us to take advantage of the opportunities for spiritual growth with which the events of our lives present us. Although these practices are extremely valuable aids, we must never confuse the means with the end. Spirituality is not about becoming an expert meditator or a master of yoga. Attempting to become a special "spiritual" person can just puff up the ego rather than help us transcend it. The Christian saint John Cassian explains:

"Fasting, vigils, the study of scripture, renouncing possessions and the world – these are the means not the end. Perfection is not found in them, but through them. It is pointless to boast about such practices when we have not achieved the love of God and our fellow humans. Those who have achieved love of God within themselves, are always mindful of God."

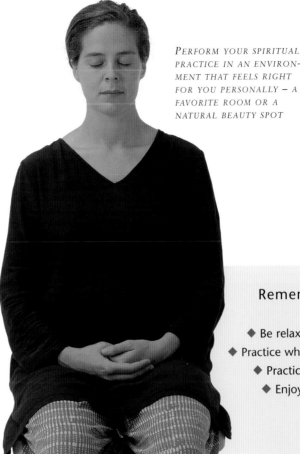

PERFORM YOUR SPIRITUAL PRACTICE IN AN ENVIRONMENT THAT FEELS RIGHT FOR YOU PERSONALLY – A FAVORITE ROOM OR A NATURAL BEAUTY SPOT

Remember to

◆ Be relaxed but alert
◆ Practice where it's peaceful
◆ Practice regularly
◆ Enjoy yourself

BEING NOT DOING

We call ourselves human *beings* not human *doings*, yet for most of us life is dominated by what we *do*. Spiritual practices are not just another thing to add to the list of "things we must do." They are an opportunity to explore what we are. Yet as Zen master Seng-t'san warns, "When we try to stop doing to achieve being, this very effort fills us with doing." Spiritual practices are a contradiction. They are something we do to attempt to transcend doing and experience BEING. Spiritual practices are like trampolines we use to bounce ourselves up into the empty space of BEING. Their whole purpose is to be left behind. When we get too busy "doing" our spiritual practices, we prevent them from launching us into the passive wonder of simply BEING.

ALREADY PERFECT

The art of spiritual practice is to do what you feel needs to be done, without becoming too "holy" about it. The secret is to remember that you are already perfect and that spirituality is a process of discovering this remarkable fact. If you could really recognize the truth of this, you would not need spiritual practices at all and would instantly awaken. Zen master Huang-po teaches:

"People perform a vast number of complex practices hoping to gain spiritual merit as countless as the grains of sand on the riverbed of the Ganges; but you are essentially already perfect in every way. Don't try to augment perfection with meaningless practice. If it's the right occasion to perform them, let practices happen. When the time has passed, let them stop."

"If you are not absolutely sure that mind is the Buddha, and if you are attached to the idea of winning merit from spiritual practices, then your thinking is misguided and not in harmony with Tao. To perform complex spiritual techniques is to progress step by step; but the eternal Buddha is not a Buddha of progressive stages. Just awaken to the one Mind, and there is absolutely nothing to be attained."

Spiritual community

*I*T CAN BE VERY HELPFUL *in maintaining and developing a spiritual practice to work with others. Most of us need spiritual friends to encourage us on our journey and to share our confusion and revelations. Just as with everyday pleasures a joy shared is often a joy doubled, so on the spiritual path having trusted companions to share our experiences can increase our insight and enjoyment. But how should we choose our spiritual friends? There are so many different spiritual groups we could join, how do we know which one is for us?*

A DISCIPLE
OF BUDDHA

CHOOSING OUR SPIRITUAL FRIENDS

Often life miraculously does the choosing for us. There is a natural law of life whereby we are attracted to those with whom we have an affinity. Sometimes, however, we may feel the need to work within a particular tradition or place ourselves under a particular teacher. In so doing, we have the opportunity to learn a great deal very quickly. But we must be cautious and listen carefully to our deepest intuitions. Spirituality is as full of charlatans as any other area of life – perhaps more so!

> **"** Look at every path closely and deliberately. Try it as many times as you think necessary. Then ask yourself, and yourself alone, one question. 'Does this path have a heart?' If it does, the path is good; if it doesn't, it is of no use. **"**
>
> DON JUAN
> MEXICAN SHAMAN

HOW SHOULD WE CHOOSE
OUR SPIRITUAL FRIENDS?

Following your heart

There are so many different spiritual traditions and practices, how do we choose which path to follow? How do we know which path will actually lead us to our destination? There is no one right way. Each one of us starts off from our own unique predicament and each one of us must find our own way up the mountain of Truth. We can certainly be guided by the wisdom of the saints and sages who have gone before us, but to decide which teachings and practices we should work with at any particular time requires us to make our own intuitive decisions about what is right for us.

Working with this encyclopedia is a good way to learn how to do this. You will not be able to fully explore all the teachings and practices it contains at any one time. So, as you look through the book, become aware of how your heart responds to what you read. Does the practice excite you? Does the teaching resonate for you? If so, embrace it. If not, move on to something that does touch you. The important thing is not to be swayed by preconceptions about what you should be doing, but to focus on those practices that feel really relevant to you.

MOUNTAINS SYMBOLIZE THE PEAK OF THE SPIRITUAL JOURNEY

AVOIDING CULTS AND CHARLATANS

Involving ourselves with the wrong people can be a waste of time or even harmful. For this reason it is sometimes recommended that we steer clear of new spiritual movements and work within tried and tested traditions. But the dangers and inadequacies associated with cults and false teachers are also common amongst groups functioning within the mainstream religions. How can we tell a genuine teacher and community of seekers from the many fanatical fakes and misguided cults? There are a number of warning signs that characterize those groups that are to be treated with suspicion and probably avoided.

ELITISM

Spirituality is about experiencing a sense of oneness with all people and all things. But many spiritual groups attract adherents by making them feel special and superior to others. Often group members are taught to believe that they have been chosen to follow the one true path. Their particular teacher is the only genuine teacher who is on a mission to save humanity. In extreme cases this is accompanied by a paranoid sense of being persecuted by a hostile world. While it is perfectly natural for spiritual teachers to demand commitment from their followers, such elitist attitudes encourage an egoistical sense of self-importance and causes deep divisions between people – the very opposite of true spirituality.

DOGMATISM

Spirituality is about transcending all concepts and beliefs, and directly experiencing the ineffable Truth for oneself. Some spiritual communities, however, require unquestioning adherence to the dogmas of the group. In extreme cases, those that question are ostracized and made

FOLLOW YOUR HEART – NOT THE HERD

MYSTICAL RAPTURE OR MASS HYSTERIA? LEARNING HOW TO DISCRIMINATE IS PART OF BECOMING SPIRITUALLY MATURE

to feel that they are unspiritual or even evil. Sometimes this is justified by teaching that the logical mind gets in the way of spiritual understanding and must be abandoned. While this is indeed an ancient and respected spiritual teaching, it is not the same thing as abandoning your own powers of discrimination and personal intuitions in favor of blind belief. Genuine spirituality does not advocate gullibility but encourages deep questioning until the seeker has genuinely found his or her own answers. Authentic teachers acknowledge that ultimately the Truth is yours already. They cannot give it to you, only help you to discover it within yourself. Those claiming that they alone can (for a fee!) impart the Truth to you are stealing your birthright and trying to sell it back to you.

66 To have friends in need is sweet,
and to share happiness,
and to have done something good
before leaving this life is sweet,
and to let go of sorrow. 99

DHAMMAPADA
BUDDHIST SCRIPTURE

❊❊❊❊

66 To each person that way is the best way that
appears easiest and appeals most. 99

RAMANA MAHARSHI
HINDU SAGE

❊❊❊❊

66 Be your own guru – your own teacher.
You have the lamp within you.
Light it and march on without fear. 99

SAI BABA
HINDU SAGE

AUTHORITARIANISM

A good way to learn anything is from someone who is already a master, and this is, of course, true of spirituality. But genuine teachers are interested in seeing their pupils graduate, not staying perpetual students. In dubious spiritual groups, however, disciples are left forever subservient to the master who is elevated to such an extent that he or she has godlike absolute authority. This does not set seekers free to realize their own unique spiritual potential, by moving on from the particular group if they feel they need to do so. Rather it builds a fanatical group of devotees around a megalomaniac. Those that do leave the fold are branded as failures or traitors rather than being allowed to follow their hearts and encouraged to find their own way, whatever that may be.

Sacred space

*T*RADITIONALLY, SPIRITUAL PRACTICES *are often performed in special places that are designated as holy, such as churches and temples or natural sacred sites. For the enlightened masters, everywhere is spiritual; for the rest of us, it can be hard to maintain this level of awareness. It is helpful, therefore, to give our spiritual practices a boost by performing them where there is already an inspiring spiritual ambience, such as a local church, temple, or shrine. It is most convenient and conducive to regular practice, however, to create our own sacred space in a special place in our home.*

CREATING A SACRED SPACE

CREATING A SACRED PLACE

Set aside a room or one corner of a room as your sacred place. If you are of a devotional disposition, create a little altar on which you can place spiritual symbols and images that you find particularly evocative. You may like to burn some incense, play devotional music, and put up pictures of the sages and spiritual teachers that you admire.

If you are of a philosophical disposition, keep here copies of your favorite spiritual books that you are studying. A noticeboard is helpful on which you can pin inspiring quotations and spiritual messages to yourself.

Perhaps you are more inclined to a Zen-type approach. In which case, you may wish to keep your sacred space very empty and uncluttered.

Make this a private space that reflects your own spiritual nature, whatever it may be. This safe haven is a place where you can retreat from the busyness of the world whenever you need to.

Use this place for your regular spiritual practices so that you begin to associate it with stillness and openheartedness. It is the launching pad for your explorations of inner space.

CREATE A SACRED SPACE THAT REFLECTS YOUR OWN SPIRITUAL NATURE

SMUDGING

Smudging is a traditional Native American method of purifying yourself and your sacred space for spiritual practice. It is best to work with a spiritual friend, first smudging each other and then your environment. You can purchase sticks of sage called "smudge sticks" to use in the ritual. Alternatively, you can place some sage, perhaps with other purifying herbs, onto some burning charcoal in a pot or shell. Burn the sage until it smolders, giving off clouds of smoke.

Ideally use an eagle's feather to circulate the smoke, because the eagle is particularly sacred to Native Americans. Otherwise choose a feather from a bird that

holds some particular significance for you. If you do not have a feather you can use your hand.

To purify one another, circulate the smoke around your partner's aura. Start from the bottom of the body and work your way up to the head. When you reach the top, flick the feathers away from you to remove the "negative energies." Do this four times, circling in a clockwise direction.

You can now smudge your sacred space, and any ritual objects within it, to purify it and enhance its spiritual ambience. Circulate the smoke in all directions while offering prayers.

> 66 I looked for Him on the Christian cross,
>
> but He was not there.
>
> I went to Hindu temples and shrines – but nothing.
>
> I visited the Ka'aba in Mecca, I did not find Him.
>
> Finally, I peered into my own heart.
>
> There, and nowhere else, was His home. 99

JALAL AL-DIN RUMI
SUFI SAGE

❦❦❦❦

> 66 I do not feel like writing verses;
>
> but as I light my perfume-burner
>
> with myrrh and jasmine incense,
>
> they suddenly burgeon from my heart,
>
> like flowers in a garden. 99

HAFIZ
SUFI SAGE

USE A SMUDGE STICK FOR PURIFICATION

Contemplation

ALL TOO OFTEN *we unquestioningly accept the norms of our culture and simply live the lives that others expect of us. The spiritual masters urge us not to follow the herd unconsciously, but to search for our own answers. We are all born alone, we will die alone, and in between we each have individual responsibility for our own lives. We can either bumble along in the semiconscious state that we think of as normal or we can wake up to the miracle of existence. We can either just accept what we've been told or transform our lives into a journey of personal discovery.*

THE JOURNEY BEGINS

CONTEMPLATING THE MYSTERIES OF EXISTENCE

Contemplation is taking the time to ask yourself the fundamental questions that have puzzled the great saints and sages throughout history: "Who am I?", "What is Life?", "What is death?". Contemplating the mysteries of existence extricates us from a habitual humdrum consciousness and helps us to understand ourselves and our lives in new ways.

CONTEMPLATION

For some people contemplation comes naturally. For others, learning to explore deep questions can at first seem a daunting prospect. Here are some general guidelines that may be helpful.

1 *Allow all extraneous thoughts to gently settle down and focus on the question you wish to contemplate.*

2 *Nurture an attitude of relaxed concentration, as if you are slowly walking around your question in a circle, eyeing it up from all sides. Don't try to force your insights but clear an inner space into which they can easily surface.*

3 *Listen carefully to hear the quiet voice of your intuitive wisdom.*

TAKE TIME TO WONDER

STUDYING SACRED TEXTS

Many traditions encourage seekers to study holy scriptures and the writings of the great saints and sages. For this to be spiritually meaningful, however, it must be more than passive indoctrination. It needs to be undertaken in a spirit of critical contemplation.

1 *Select a passage from a spiritual text that particularly attracts you. You could choose one of the many quotations in this book. It doesn't matter if you don't immediately understand it, as long as you find it intriguing or inspiring.*

2 *Read the passage a number of times and then sit quietly and think through exactly what it means to you. What is it really saying? What is its relevance to your life?*

3 *The language and style of most sacred texts reflect the time and culture from which they come. Once you feel you have understood what the passage you are contemplating means, consider how you would express this meaning in your own unique way in a modern context.*

DON'T BELIEVE SOMETHING JUST BECAUSE IT IS WRITTEN IN A BOOK

66 Just as someone who looks at the sun
cannot avoid filling his eyes with light,
so someone who always intently contemplates
his own heart cannot fail to be illuminated. 99

ST. HESYCHIOS THE PRIEST
CHRISTIAN SAGE

❊❊❊❊

66 Mind itself is both the cause of bondage
and the means to liberation. 99

AJJA
HINDU SAGE

A HINDU VISION OF THE OMNIPRESENCE OF GOD

Prayer

RAYER IS ONE *of the simplest and most common spiritual practices. Many children are introduced to formal spirituality by being taught to talk to God in their prayers. Prayer is a way of cultivating a remembrance of God. In prayers we can give thanks for all the blessings of our lives, so that we don't take them for granted. In prayer we can share our fears and hopes and needs with the Higher Power that sustains us.*

ASKING FOR GUIDANCE

HOLY LONGING

Prayers express our yearning for spiritual awakening. The many beautiful traditional prayers poetically entice the Higher Power to grace us with a blissful revelation of its constant presence. In prayer we humble ourselves before something greater. Christians kneel before images of Christ. Buddhist bow before statues of the Buddha. Muslim face Mecca and prostrate themselves on their prayer mats. The Christian mystic Brother Lawrence recommends, "Hold yourself in prayer before God like a dumb and paralytic beggar at a rich man's gate."

MERGING THE MIND WITH THE HIGHER POWER

Prayer is more than petitioning an all-powerful Deity with our personal desires. It is an age-old spiritual technique to merge the mind with the Higher Power to which we are addressing our prayers. Like repeating the word "silence" to draw our attention to the silence, prayer is about using words to bring to our awareness the quiet stillness of God.

MUSLIMS AT PRAYER IN DUBAI

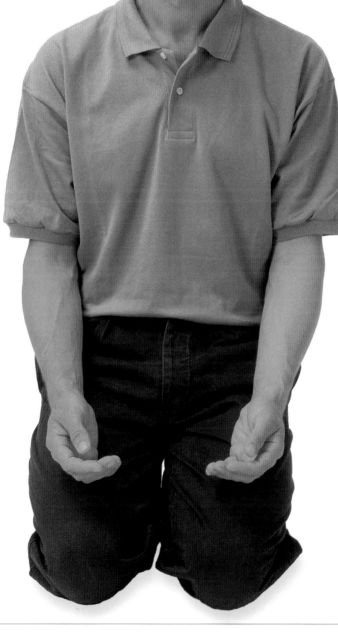

SILENT COMMUNION

To fully enter the highest stage of prayer, the spiritual masters teach that we must go beyond using words altogether and commune with the Great Mystery in silence. As the Christian saint Isaac the Syrian explains, "True wisdom is gazing at God. Gazing at God is silence of thoughts." The alchemist and Christian sage Albertus Magnus teaches that if we still the mind completely in prayer, we will know the mind itself to be God.

JUST GREAT TO BE TOGETHER

Silent prayer, sometimes known as meditation, has been practiced by saints and sages from all the spiritual traditions of the world. It may sound less personal than verbal prayer, but actually it is more intimate. Like the relaxed silence between two familiar lovers, anything said would just break the spell of the unspoken closeness. The Hindu sage Swami Chetananda describes this state in beautiful everyday language when he writes:

❝ When you pray, shut the door of the senses against all fantasies and thoughts. Nothing pleases God more than a mind free from distractions. Such a mind is transformed into God, for it can think of nothing, understand nothing, love nothing, except God; seeing other creatures and itself only in God. ❞

ALBERTUS MAGNUS
CHRISTIAN SAGE

❝ When you are with someone you love very much, you can talk and it is pleasant, but the reality is not in the conversation. It is in simply being together. Meditation is the highest form of prayer. In it you are so close to God that you don't need to say a thing – it is just great to be together. ❞

SWAMI CHETANANDA
HINDU SAGE

Moses and the Shepherd

One day Moses overheard a humble shepherd praying to God. The shepherd's tone was relaxed and familiar as he told God how he wanted to pick the lice off of him, to wash his clothes, to kiss his hands and feet. He ended his prayer with "When I think of You all I can say is Ahhhhh!" Moses was appalled and exclaimed, "Do you realize you are talking to the Creator of Heaven and Earth, not to your old uncle?!" The shepherd repented of his ignorance and wandered sadly off into the desert.

Suddenly there was a great voice from the heavens rebuking Moses, saying, "What to you seems wrong is right for him. One man's poison is another man's honey. Purity and impurity, sloth and diligence – what do these matter to me? I am above all that. Ways of worship cannot be put in ranks as better and worse. It is all praise and it is all right. It is the worshiper who is glorified by worship – not I. I don't listen to the words. I look inside at the humility. Only that low and open emptiness is real. Forget language – I want burning, burning! Be friends with this fire. Burn up your ideas and your special words."

SUFI TEACHING STORY

A SHEPHERD SPEAKS TO MOSES ON SINAI

SPEAKING TO THE SILENCE

There are two ways of approaching verbal prayer. One is to recite prayers that you know and love. These could be famous prayers, such as the Christian "Lord's Prayer," or you could look through books from different religious traditions and find prayers that appeal to you. You can read these prayers out loud or inwardly, or recite them from memory with eyes closed.

Focus on what the words really mean to you. Don't just repeat them by rote. It is not the words that matter, but your sincere intention to reach out to the Higher Power.

The other way is to sit quietly with eyes closed and let your own words emerge spontaneously. Don't feel inhibited; no one is listening except the Great Mystery, and it loves you unconditionally. Reach deep inside and bare your heart. Share your worries and fears, your hopes and aspirations, your confusion and questions – but remember also to share your gratitude and wonder.

PRAYING IS MORE THAN JUST REPEATING CERTAIN WORDS

Don't forget that prayer is about using words to reach the mystical silence. So, having offered up your prayers, let them go and commune with the stillness. It is in this profound quiet that our prayers are truly answered.

---

66 It is shameful to abandon our conversations with God to think of some trifling nonsense. 99

BROTHER LAWRENCE
CHRISTIAN SAGE

✱✱✱✱

66 Do not pray for anything in particular for yourselves. How do you know what is good for you? 99

PYTHAGORAS
PAGAN SAGE

66 Prayer means the shedding of thought. 99

EVAGRIUS PONTUS
CHRISTIAN SAGE

✱✱✱✱

66 Is not silence the very voice of Great Spirit? 99

BLACK ELK
NATIVE AMERICAN SAGE

Meditation

MOST SPIRITUAL TRADITIONS *teach meditation in one form or another. Meditation is a broad term that covers many diverse techniques that focus the mind to nurture spiritual realization. Sitting still in a quiet environment, often with eyes closed, practitioners turn their attention away from the outer world of the senses and look inward to discover the nature of Consciousness itself. To help them avoid getting caught up in distracting thoughts, they fix their attention on an object of meditation. Often this is simply the breath as it passes in and out of the body.*

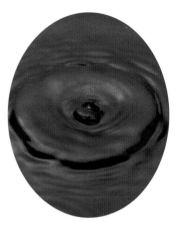

FIND THE STILL CENTER

BREATH

The breath is a perfect focus for meditation because it is what is keeping us alive moment to moment. We are always breathing so we can mediate on the breath at any time. Breath also reminds us of our essential unity, because we all breath the same air. Breath only becomes "our" breathe when it is contained within our lungs. It comes from the shared atmosphere and returns to the shared atmosphere. Breathing thus reminds us that, although we appear to be separate, in fact all things are One.

THE CLEAR BLUE SKY OF CONSCIOUSNESS

Buddhist meditation teachers often compare Consciousness to a clear blue sky across which thoughts pass like clouds. Our thoughts may be unpleasant, like menacing storm clouds, or they may be inspired and beautiful, like fluffy summer clouds. But all thoughts clutter the emptiness of Consciousness. Meditation is a technique for removing our attention from the clouds and becoming aware of the spacious clarity of the sky. It is a method to help us disengage from our habitual preoccupation with thoughts and become conscious of the Consciousness within which they arise.

MEDITATION CLEARS THE CLOUDS OF THOUGHT

THE EMPTY MIND

We are all thought addicts, so it is very easy to pay attention to every passing thought. By concentrating the attention on the breath, or some other point of focus, it is easier for the meditator not to be caught up in the constant chatter of the mind. Just as you cannot pick up something if your hands are already full, if your attention is already fully occupied you cannot give it to anything else. By not paying attention to our thoughts, they begin to settle down, just as the mud in a dirty puddle settles slowly if the water is no longer agitated. When this happens, the mind, like the puddle, becomes clear and transparent, and the meditator experiences the nature of empty Consciousness. This is our essential identity – our Atman, our Buddha-Nature, our eternal Spirit.

The Monkey Mind

Sitting in meditation reveals how restless the mind is. To begin with you may feel very agitated. The mind may start telling you that meditation is a complete waste of time. You may suddenly become accosted with seemingly urgent demands to abandon your practice and get on with some important task that previously had felt inconsequential. You may experience terrible boredom or overwhelming drowsiness. Such reactions can seem like failure, but they are only a transitory stage in the practice of meditation, which demonstrates just how dominated we are by what the Hindus call "the monkey mind."

THE SIKH GURU RAM DAS

RELATIONSHIP WITH THE MIND

The mind is an excellent servant but a lousy master. By stilling our mental babble through persevering in meditation, a more appropriate relationship with the mind can be nurtured in which we do not let it rule us. The chattering will not immediately simply fall silent, but it can soon become like a mildly irritating radio playing in a distant room to which we are no longer listening, leaving us free to bathe in the stillness.

BREATH MEDITATION

Breath meditation is an ubiquitous meditation technique. In some traditions it is important to adopt a certain body posture, such as sitting cross-legged with an upright back in the "lotus position." This encourages an alert awareness, but is not essential. It is fine to sit in any position that makes you relaxed and comfortable without encouraging feelings of drowsiness. To begin with, sit for about 20 minutes at a time.

1 *Close your eyes and focus your attention on your breath as it rises and falls.*

2 *As thoughts and feelings arise, let them come and go, like clouds passing across the empty sky of your awareness.*

3 *If you become caught up in thoughts, immediately return your attention to your breath.*

Don't be disheartened if you become distracted. Meditation is not about forcing yourself to stop thinking. The more you try to do this, the more agitated you will become. Let the mind relax and accept whatever happens. Through constant practice a state of inner peace will begin to arise naturally.

FOCUS ON YOUR BREATH

CANDLE MEDITATION

A simple way to begin exploring the power of meditation is to contemplate a candle.

1 *Sit comfortably in a relaxing, dark environment. Place a lit candle before you and focus your attention on the flame.*

2 *Look intensely at the candlelight and listen to the silence. Nurture an open, receptive, alert state of awareness.*

3 *If distracting thoughts arise, don't follow them, just allow them to pass away. Don't try too hard, but let the mind naturally come to a rest.*

66 If the power to think is a remarkable gift, then the power not to think is even more so. 99

SRI AUROBINDO
HINDU SAGE

❊❊❊❊

66 Be empty. Be still.

Watch everything just come and go.

Emerging from the Source – returning to the Source.

This is the way of Nature.

This is the fulfilment of your destiny.

Know that which never changes.

This is enlightenment. 99

LAO TZU
TAOIST SAGE

❊❊❊❊

66 Prayer is breathing in and breathing out the one breath of the universe. 99

HILDEGARD DE BINGEN
CHRISTIAN MYSTIC

❊❊❊❊

66 The essential nature of mind is the background to the whole of life and death, like the sky which folds the universe in its embrace. 99

SOGYAL RINPOCHE
TIBETAN LAMA

Mantras

A Chinese Prayer Wheel

A *MANTRA IS A word or phrase used as an object of meditation. By constantly repeating a mantra, either out loud or to themselves, practitioners distract themselves from their restless thoughts and enter a meditative state of awareness. A common mantra is to repeat one of the names of God. Traditionally, a spiritual teacher gives a student a mantra tailored to his or her specific needs, but any word or phrase that has spiritual resonance for the individual seeker can be used as a mantra.*

MAGICAL WORDS

In our culture, words are seen as merely the tools of communication, with no significance of their own; but in many spiritual traditions, words are regarded as having magical properties. We take language for granted, so it is easy to overlook what a miracle it is that one person can articulate a sound that conveys his or her private thoughts to someone else. Words bring to mind the object to which they refer. In many spiritual traditions, therefore, to say the word "God" is to invoke the divine presence. This is the basis of the spiritual technique of mantra repetition.

THE PATH OF NAMES

Mantra meditation is usually associated with Hinduism and Buddhism, but it is actually an ubiquitous technique found in all traditions. Muslims repeat "Allah" or one of the other "Ninety-nine Most Beautiful Names of God." Didochus, a 5th-century Christian bishop, prayed by repeating "Jesus Christ, Son of God," as he inhaled and "have mercy upon me, a sinner" as he exhaled. The Jewish Cabalist Abulafia, practiced a form of mantra meditation that he called "The Path of Names." He believed that whoever succeeded in losing himself or herself in the names of God would receive spiritual revelations.

THE PRIMAL SOUND

A powerful Hindu mantra used by millions of spiritual practitioners through the ages is "OM," pronounced "A-U-M." In Hinduism, OM is regarded as the primal sound of the universe, and repeating it connects you to the underlying vibration of life. OM is a word beyond meaning that designates the ineffable Oneness that is beyond intellectual comprehension.

REPETITIVE ACTION

Often mantra meditation is accompanied by repetitive actions to aid concentration. Tibetan Buddhists spin a prayer wheel while repeating a mantra such as "Aum Mani Padme Hum," which is also written on a piece of paper at the center of the wheel. Christian mystics repeat a one-line prayer while fingering rosary beads. In the same way, Hindus use a string of beads called a "mala." Every time practitioners repeat the mantra they pass a bead between their fingers. The beads are linked by one thread, which reminds them that all separate things are united by the Oneness of God.

ROSARY BEADS

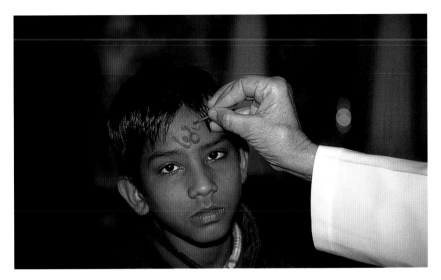

A HINDU PRIEST WRITES OM ON A BOY'S FOREHEAD

Hari Krishna

66 Hari Krishna, Hari Krishna, Hari Hari, Krishna Krishna.
Hari Rama, Hari Rama, Rama Rama, Krishna Krishna 99

The Hindu "Hari Krishna" mantra can now be heard sung by orange-clad devotees in most major cities in the West. These followers of the god Krishna are members of the Krishna Consciousness Movement founded in 1965 by the Indian guru Swami Prabhupada. He was inspired by a 16th-century Bengali saint named Caitanya. Caitanya was an ecstatic mystic who was renowned for his devotional excesses – crying, singing, shouting, dancing, climbing trees, and jumping up and down while intoxicated with divine love. Eventually he drowned in a holy river while in a fit of ecstasy. In the tradition he inspired, devotees dance and chant the names of God with mounting intensity, sometimes in procession through the streets, until they lose themselves in rapture.

*DEVOTEES DANCE THROUGH
A LONDON STREET*

Traditional Mantras

Aum Mani Padme Hum

The All is a precious jewel
in the lotus flower
that blooms in my heart.

Tibetan Buddhist

Gaté, Gaté,
Paragaté,
Parasamgaté,
Bodhi Svaha.

Beyond, beyond,
Beyond the great beyond,
Beyond even the thought of beyond,
Homage to Thee!

Tibetan Buddhist

Sri Ram, Jai Ram,
Jai, Jai Ram

Praise to God, Hail to God,
Hail, Hail to God.

Hindu

Aditya Hridayam Punyam
Sarv Shatru Beena Shenam

All evil vanishes from life for those
who keep the Sun in their hearts.

Hindu

OM Namah Shivaya

Om! I bow to God.

Hindu

MANTRA MEDITATION

Mantra meditation can be silently practiced in the mind at any time, but to begin with it is best to put aside a period for formal mantra meditation. You can use any word, phrase, or sound as a mantra, but it is best to choose something that has personal relevance. You may like to repeat one of the traditional mantras given in this section, or you could use a short phrase such as "God is Love" or simply "Love." You may choose to use the traditional Hindu mantra "OM" – pronounced "A-U-M."

1 Sit still and relaxed with eyes closed and repeat out loud the mantra you have chosen.

2 Focus your mind completely on the mantra, and whenever it strays come back to constant repetition.

3 Don't worry if you get bored with your mantra, that is part of the practice. It is a barrier you need to go through. It means you have reached the point where your conscious mind is no longer interested in the novelty of using a mantra and wants some new stimulus. If you stick with your practice your mind will give up altogether and become very quiet.

OM is a beautiful mantra to practice with spiritual friends because your voices will resonate together, bringing you into wordless communion with each other. Breathe deeply and slowly. On the exhalation slowly intone A-U-M with a low and constant voice until your lungs are completely emptied.

FOCUS ON A MANTRA

66 By repetition of holy mantras the sinner is released from guilt. 99

LAWS OF MANU
HINDU SCRIPTURE

66 Invoke the all-embracing Name, which is Allah, Allah, Allah. But don't violate this remembrance by letting your tongue pronounce His Name while something else is in your heart. Let your heart speak and your ear witness, until the speaker becomes your true Self. 99

AHMAD IBN ATA'ALLAH
SUFI SAGE

Koans

CONTEMPLATING A KOAN *is a form of meditation practiced by some schools of Zen. Koans are Zen riddles. A famous traditional koan is "What is the sound of one hand clapping?" Such crazy questions cannot be solved with the powers of the rational mind. They force us to go beyond our habitual ways of thinking. Their paradoxical nature creates an unbearable mental tension that can only be resolved by a spontaneous breakthrough of intuitive insight. Students may present their master with any number of clever responses, but a koan is not answered by words. It is answered by a transformation of consciousness. When the student finally answers the koan with his or her being rather than the mind, any answer will be the right answer – even something completely absurd.*

ONE HAND
CLAPPING?

MU!

"Mu!" is a famous traditional koan that literally translates as "not." "Mu!" means "Anything you can think is not the answer." "Mu!" demands "Abandon your conceptual understanding and directly experience What-Is." "Mu!" is neither affirming something nor negating it. "Mu!" is declaring that both "yes" and "no" are too limited to be the answer. "Mu!" is proclaiming "Unask that question!" "Mu!" points to a direct experience of the Oneness in which there are no questions.

MEDITATING ON "MU!"

You can choose any koan as an object of meditation, but "Mu!" is perhaps the most powerful. Both in silent meditation and while going about your daily life, confront all that you believe with "Mu!"

MEDITATE DURING
DAILY ROUTINES

Do you think you know who you are?

Mu!

Do you think you don't know who you are?

Mu!

Go beyond every "yes" and "no" to the Oneness of Mu!

Mu!

A Red-hot Ball of Iron

Zen master Ekai, who was suddenly enlightened upon hearing the monastery drum after years meditating on "Mu!", gave the following advice to his students:

"Concentrate on 'Mu' with your whole self, every bone and pore, until it makes you a solid lump of doubt. Day and night, without stopping, keep digging into it. Don't view it as 'nothingness' or as 'being' or as 'nonbeing.' Make it a red-hot ball of iron that you have swallowed down and want to vomit up – but just can't. Forget all illusionary thoughts and feelings that are dear to you. After some time of making this effort, 'Mu!' will bear fruit and, quite spontaneously, inside and out will become one. You will end up like a dumb man who has awoken from dreaming. You will know yourself – but only for yourself. 'Mu!' will suddenly explode, shaking the earth and opening the heavens."

Who Am I?

According to Zen, our innate Buddha-Nature is obscured by the cacophony of opinions that fill our minds all the time. We don't discover who we really are, because we are too busy believing our opinions about who we think we are. Asking "Who am I?" is a powerful koan because, although we may start off presuming we know the answer, the deeper we contemplate the question the more we become aware that everything we think we are is only a thought that we are thinking! But who is the thinker? Zen teaches us to contemplate this question relentlessly until the mind implodes with the tension of intense and futile mental investigation. When this happens, Consciousness naturally becomes still and empty and our "Buddha-Nature" – our true identity – is silently obvious.

BUDDHA AT THE SHWEDAGON PAGODA
IN RANGOON, MYANMAR

WHO ARE YOU WHEN YOUR MIND IS STILL?

This exercise, based on a traditional Zen practice, will help you explore the power of contemplating koans with a spiritual friend.

1 *Choose a profound question as a koan, which you will ask your partner. A good one to start with is "Who are you?" Later you could also try questions such as "What is life about?" or "What is love?" or "What is important to you?"*

2 *Sit opposite each other so that you can meet each other's gaze. Let yourselves become relaxed and alert.*

3 *One of you starts by asking the other the chosen koan. The other should then spontaneously respond with any answers that come to mind. In response to "Who are you?", for example, you may begin by saying your name and occupation – the normal superficial sort of things we tell people at parties!*

4 *If there is a pause, the questioner should again repeat the question "Who are you?" – encouraging a fresh response.*

5 *Go on like this for five minutes, then swap roles. At the end of the next five minutes, swap back again, and so on. The longer you keep this up the better.*

6 *Don't think about the process, just keep asking the same question and giving whatever answers come to mind. Once you have exhausted all your ideas about who you think you are, you may start resenting the constant probing, or you may find yourself giving clever "spiritual" answers. When these too have all been said, you may begin giving new and truly spontaneous replies, which may be extremely illuminating.*

7 *Eventually you may dry up altogether and find yourself without a clue as to who you really are. Don't fight this feeling. Allow your mind to become completely silent to reveal your own innate Buddha-Nature. This may not happen, but that doesn't matter. The process itself will at least tell you much about who you think you are.*

Remember that there is no correct answer to a koan, because it is a search for transformation, not information. The search is over only when the mind runs out of potential answers and everything just is.

*PRACTICE KOANS WITH A
SPIRITUAL FRIEND*

66 While striving to catch the butterfly of Zen
in the net of reason
we must know that the task is hopeless. 99

CHRISTMAS HUMPHREYS
ZEN TEACHER

❊❊❊❊

66 What was your original face
before your parents were born? 99

ZEN KOAN

❊❊❊❊

66 True meditation is making everything – coughing,
swallowing, waving, movement and stillness, speaking
and acting, good and evil, fame and shame, loss and
gain, right and wrong – into one single koan. 99

HAKUIN
ZEN MASTER

❊❊❊❊

66 Don't you realize that if you simply have no
concepts and no anxiety, you'll see the Buddha
standing before you. 99

HUANG-PO
ZEN MASTER

ZEN CONTEMPLATION

Visualization

VISUALIZATION IS A *form of meditation that uses the power of the imagination to encourage particular spiritual states of being. Symbols and images are the language of the deep mind. Visualization is one way of using this language to communicate with the unconscious. The most complex visualization meditations are found in the Buddhist Tantric traditions in which practitioners visualize gods, goddesses, or celestial Buddhas, and invoke the powers they represent to gain spiritual insight. A much simpler form of visualization meditation, commonly found in the New Age movement, is to encourage deep relaxation by imagining oneself by a calm ocean or some other beautiful natural environment.*

THE HINDU
GOD SHIVA

Being as Expansive as God

Among the writings attributed to the ancient Egyptian sage Hermes Trismegistus is a visualization exercise that teaches us to come to know God by imagining ourselves to be like God – present everywhere and always:

To know God we must share his identity,
for only like can truly know like.

Leave behind the material world,
and imagine yourself immeasurably expansive.
Rise out of time to eternity.
Then you will know God.
Believe that for you too nothing is impossible.
Imagine that you are immortal
and learned in every art and science.

Imagine yourself at home
in the haunts of every living creature.
Make yourself higher than the highest,
and deeper than the depths.
Embrace within yourself all opposites ,
heat and cold, hard and fluid.
Think yourself everywhere at once –
on land – at sea – in heaven.
Imagine yourself unborn in the womb,
yet also young, and old, and already dead –
and in the world beyond the grave.

See that everything coexists
within consciousness.
All times and all places.
All things of all shapes and sizes.

Then you will know God.

*JEWISH MYSTICS DEVELOPED
VISUALIZATION EXERCISES
BASED ON THE SCRIPTURES*

EXPLORING CHAMBERS
OF CONSCIOUSNESS

Jewish mystics practiced a system of visualization meditations called "Hekhalot," which means "chambers" or "palaces." The practitioners imagined themselves passing through a series of seven inner chambers, representing different spiritual states of consciousness, connected by a series of bridges and guarded by angelic forces. Once inside a particular chamber they received spontaneous visions that revealed the secret wisdom of that particular inner state. The Jewish sage Hai Gaon explains the practice:

"You must fast for a specific number of days. You must place your head between your knees whispering softly to yourself the while certain praises of God with your face toward the ground. As a result you will gaze in the innermost recesses of your heart and it will seem as if you see the seven halls with your own eyes, moving from hall to hall to observe that which is therein to be found."

PSYCHIC ABILITIES

This practice is similar to Eastern yogic practices in which practitioners use visualization to awaken the seven chakras. Like their Indian counterparts, the Jewish mystics claimed that experiencing these different levels of consciousness brought psychic powers, such as the ability to foresee the future and remember past lives.

THE GUARDIAN OF THE CAVERN

Practice this visualization exercise with a spiritual friend, taking turns to read the instructions slowly while the other person closes his or her eyes and follows the suggestions. Pause long enough to allow your partner to visualize what you are describing before offering the next image.

As you follow the instructions, allow the images to come into your mind, but don't force anything. Immediately your visualization is complete, make a note of the things you saw and heard in your imagination so that you can contemplate them and discuss their significance with your friend.

This visualization exercise takes us into an underground cavern, a common symbol of the unconscious or deep mind. Here we meet a wise guardian who symbolizes our innate wisdom.

1 *Breath slowly and deeply. Completely relax your body and mind.*

2 *Image yourself at the entrance to a cave. Walk into the cave and look around you. What sort of a cave is it?*

3 *There is light glowing in a distant recess of the cave. Walk toward the light. The cave is getting smaller and narrower. Squeeze through until you come into a brightly lit cavern full of candles. The walls are lined with sparkling precious jewels. Look around you. What else can you see?*

4 *At the center of the cavern is a mysterious pool of water, and by the pool stands an old man. This is the guardian of the cavern who is here to teach you. Ask him humbly for a message from your deep Self and listen carefully to what he has to say.*

VISUALIZE THE
CANDLELIT CAVERN

THE SANCTUARY

5 *The pool reaches down forever into the depths of your true Self. Look into the pool and allow an image to appear in the still waters. This is a symbolic message that can teach you something about yourself and the life predicaments you are facing at the moment.*

6 *Now thank the guardian for his teachings and make your way back out of the cave into the warm sunlight. Then when you feel ready, open your eyes.*

Write down the teachings you were given by the guardian of the cavern, the image in the pool and anything else that particularly struck you during your imaginative journey. Then share your experiences with your spiritual friend and ask for his or her insights and observations.

You can use your experiences as a focus for personal meditation. Or you may wish to revisit this magical cavern on your own now that you know the way. It is your secret inner sanctuary and you can journey there for healing and teachings whenever you wish.

66 God says 'I appear uniquely to each of my servants. What each one imagines me to be, I become. Listen my servants, I am enclosed within these images.' 99

JALAL AL-DIN RUMI
SUFI SAGE

❃❃❃❃

66 Imagine Brahman as a sea without shores. 99

RAMAKRISHNA
HINDU SAINT

❃❃❃❃

66 I love the visualization of standing at the seashore looking out at the vast ocean and knowing that this ocean is the abundance that is available to me. 99

LOUISE L. HAY
NEW AGE TEACHER

PRINCE SIDDHARTHA, WHO LATER BECAME BUDDHA, SEES THE FOUR OMENS.

Meditation in movement

MEDITATION IS NOT *about withdrawing from the world to achieve peace of mind. It is about discovering a still center within from which to live with equanimity in the midst of all the comings and goings of life. Spiritual techniques that teach meditation in movement help us to find inner calm without closing our eyes and being still. They assist us to integrate meditation into all aspects of our lives, so that we are just as mindful when performing our daily chores as when we are focused on a formal spiritual practice. Whatever we happen to be doing, being in meditation helps us to enter the present moment fully and become aware of the continual miracle of existence.*

MEDITATE DURING DAILY LIFE

WITNESSING OUR ACTIONS

On its deepest level, meditation in movement helps us become a detached witness of "our" actions and achieve the state the Taoists call "wu wei" or "no doer." Focused in this state of awareness, the sages understand that all of "their" actions are in reality happening to them. They are not the "doer" but the observing consciousness. We all allow basic bodily functions, such as digestion, to occur without our "doing" them. If we had to think about them, it would be a great burden. The sages who have merged with Tao allow all of "their" actions to flow spontaneously and effortlessly from their being without any sense of intention or personal will.

WU-WEI – "NONACTION"

The One-legged Dragon and the Centipede

A one-legged dragon named Hui asked a centipede, "How do you manage all those legs? I can hardly manage one!" The centipede replied, "As a matter of fact, I do not manage my legs."
In the same way that the centipede lets his legs manage themselves, the sage allows all of "his" actions to naturally "manage themselves."

TAOIST TEACHING STORY

WALKING MEDITATION

The simplest form of meditation in movement is the Buddhist practice of walking meditation. During long periods of spiritual practice, Buddhists alternate between sitting meditation and walking meditation. But you can practice walking meditation on its own, either in a formal setting or while you are out taking a stroll.

1 *Walk extremely slowly and steadily – the slower the better.*

2 *Concentrate your mind on the process of walking that you usually perform completely unconsciously. Notice how you move your weight from one leg to the other; how you begin to lift one foot until it is in the air, move it forward in space and place your heel down, and then your whole foot, before transferring your weight.*

3 *Try not to let your attention stray from the steady rhythm created by your walking. If you concentrate deeply, you can even become aware of a more subtle level still – the inner intention to shift your weight and then the movement itself, the inner intention to place your foot, and then the placing of the foot, and so on.*

MEDITATION IN MOTION

MIRRORING

Mirroring is a meditation in movement exercise performed by students of the Chinese martial art called Tai Chi Chuan. It can help you to develop a spacious, meditative awareness in which you start to perceive directly with the body, rather than through mental processing.

1 *This exercise is performed with a spiritual friend. Decide which of you will begin by being the active partner and which the passive partner. Stand about six feet (two meters) away from your partner, facing each other.*

2 *The active partner moves his or her body extremely slowly, starting with simple movements, such as raising a hand or leg. At first move only one limb at a time, then begin to move the body as a whole. Never turn around so that you cannot see your partner.*

3 *The passive partner should mimic these movements as if he or she were a mirror. For example, if the active partner raises the left arm, the passive partner raises his or her right arm in the same manner. The passive partner should let the mind be still and empty so that the body instinctively responds to what it sees, rather than via mental processing. The more thoughts, the slower and less accurate the mirroring will be.*

4 *At first the passive partner may try to shift attention rapidly around the whole of the active partner's body to try to take in all the movements. But the passive partner will soon find that this slows things down too much and he or she cannot react quickly enough. The answer is to rest the attention in the chest area and cultivate an ambient awareness that extends to all perimeters of the body at once.*

5 *Once you have become competent at mirroring, you may like to make the movements faster and more complex, but don't do this too soon or your partner may feel inadequate and become discouraged.*

6 *After about five minutes the active partner should come to rest in any position he or she chooses and say "change." This is the signal for the previously passive partner to start leading and the previously active partner to begin mirroring.*

MIRRORING
NURTURES SPACIOUS
AWARENESS

" In Buddhist meditation we do not struggle for the kind of enlightenment that will happen five or ten years from now. We practice so that each moment of our lives becomes real life. The same kind of mindfulness can be practiced when we eat breakfast, or when we hold a child in our arms, or hug our mother, or our husband, or our friend. "

THICH NHAT HANH
BUDDHIST SAGE

❅❅❅❅

" Meditation in movement is a hundred, a thousand, a million times superior to meditation at rest. "

ZEN SAYING

❅❅❅❅

" Think of moving things as stationary and still things as in motion, then movement and rest will both disappear. "

SENG-T'SAN
ZEN MASTER

❅❅❅❅

" Try not to focus your mind anywhere in particular, but rather let it fill all of your body. Let it flow through your whole being. "

TAKUAN
ZEN MASTER

Tai Chi Chuan

*T*AI CHI CHUAN, *often simply known as Tai Chi, is a Chinese martial art that embodies the paradoxical principle of Taoism that the secret to great strength is great softness. Just as water can wear away the hardest rocks, so Tai Chi uses the power of relaxation, rather than force, to overcome an opponent. Most people practice Tai Chi for its great health benefits rather than as a means of self-defense. It was invented by monks and can be used as a form of meditation in movement. It is said that through the practice of Tai Chi it is possible to gain the flexibility of a small child, the strength of a lumberjack, and the peacefulness of a sage.*

A SYMBOL OF STABILITY

FLUID YET ROOTED

Tai Chi is very popular in China with people of all ages as a form of exercise that brings health and harmony to body, mind, and soul. Practitioners slowly move their relaxed bodies in carefully prescribed ways so that each position flows effortlessly from the one before. The aim of Tai Chi is to be as fluid as a mountain stream yet as solid and rooted in the earth as an old tree. In Chinese philosophy, the body and mind are not thought of as separate but as a unified body–mind. By relaxing and pacifying the body, Tai Chi also relaxes and pacifies the mind. Tai Chi not only exercises the muscles and internal organs of the physical body, but also energizes the subtle body that surrounds it. Great masters of Tai Chi are said to be able to control this subtle energy or "chi" in remarkable ways and so perform seemingly magical acts.

EFFORTLESS ACTION

On its deepest level, Tai Chi is a spiritual practice whose goal is achieving oneness with the Tao. Although practitioners may look as if they are carefully controlling their movements, the aim is to be so relaxed that the movements effortlessly flow through the body. In this way the practitioner may experience the Taoist goal of spontaneous action known as "wu wei."

PEOPLE PRACTICING TAI CHI IN SHANGHAI, CHINA

LETTING GO OF THE ARMS

To master Tai Chi it is necessary to study with a competent teacher, but there are simple exercises you can play with to get a taste of the Tai Chi experience. Most people are permanently tense. Tai Chi is about deep relaxation. This exercise, which focuses on completely relaxing the arms, helps you learn the art of letting go. It should be performed with a friend.

1 Choose one partner to be passive and one to be active. The passive partner should stand completely still with eyes closed and legs together and slightly bent at the knees. He or she should focus attention on the breath and let the arms hang by the side, utterly limp like strands of heavy rope.

2 The active partner should now gently lift one of the passive partner's arms into his or her hands and slowly move it up and down and from side to side. Both partners should pay close attention to how the arms feels. Is it limp and relaxed or is the passive partner holding on to it?

3 The passive partner may react to the movement of his or her arm by clenching the muscles to "help" take the weight of the arm. If the passive partner find this is happening, he or she should breath out all the tension with a loud sigh and let the arm go into the partner's hands.

4 If the active partner can feel that he or she is not taking all the weight and the passive partner seems unaware of this, the active partner may compassionately point this out and encourage the passive partner to relax.

5 At first the active partner should avoid lifting the arm too high because this makes it more difficult to let go. Once the passive partner seems to be generally relaxed, however, the active partner can begin to move the arm to positions where the passive partner still begins to tense. This will show where the passive partner is still holding and give an opportunity to deepen the relaxation.

6 Having performed this exercise with one arm for about five minutes, repeat with the other arm, then swap roles.

LEARN TO LET GO

STICKY HANDS

Sticky Hands is a traditional Tai Chi exercise that teaches meditative concentration, spacious awareness, and the ability to respond intuitively. It is practiced with a partner. Sticky Hands should be played like a game with a mixture of serious intent and a light-hearted sense of fun.

1 *Choose one partner to be passive and one to be active. The passive partner should close the eyes and stand with feet shoulder-width apart, knees slightly bent, and arms relaxed. The active partner should keep the eyes open and place the palm of one of the passive partner's hands on the top of one of his or her own hands. The passive partner should let the palm rest here – not too heavily not too lightly – with the body–mind relaxed but alert.*

2 *The active partner should now begin slowly moving his or her hand. The passive partner's job is to "stick" to the active partner's hand, so that no matter where it moves the passive partner's hand does not fall off.*

3 *As the exercise develops, the active partner may begin walking around. The passive partner will now have to move the whole body to remain "stuck" to the active partner's hand. The active partner must make sure not to lead the passive partner into any obstacles, and the passive partner must relax and trust the active partner completely.*

4 *To perform this exercise effectively, the passive partner must learn to sense instinctively the slightest movements in the active partner's hand and how it relates to the rest of the body movement. If the passive partner tries to think about what is happening and anticipate the active partner's movements, his or her hand will soon fall off. If this happens, the passive partner should not open the eyes. The active partner should simply pick up the passive partner's hand and start again.*

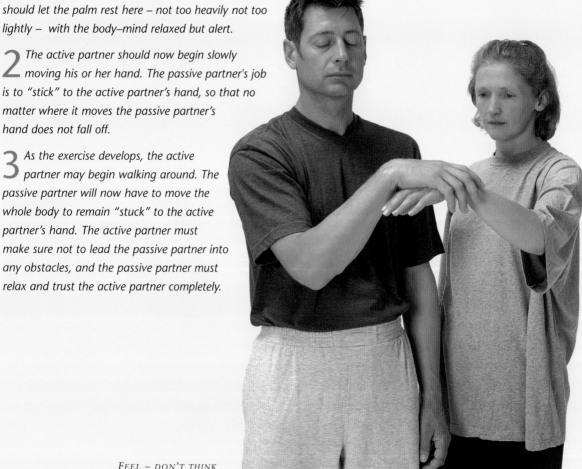

MAINTAIN CONTACT AT ALL TIMES

FEEL – DON'T THINK

5 At first the active partner will easily be able to lose the passive partner. But to do this would be discouraging. Instead, the active partner should compassionately help the passive partner gain confidence and develop a meditative, responsive state of awareness. Then the active partner may begin to make the task more difficult.

6 Having performed this exercise for a few minutes with one hand, change hands and repeat, then swap roles.

FOLLOW YOUR
PARTNER'S MOVEMENTS

66 Softness is harder than hardness.

Weakness is stronger than strength. 99

LAO TZU
TAOIST SAGE

❋❋❋❋

66 When you were born you were soft and supple.

When you die you will be hard and stiff.

Green shoots are fresh and full of vitality.

Dead plants are withered and dry.

Hard and stiff go with death.

Soft and supple go with life. 99

LAO TZU

❋❋❋❋

66 Have complete fluidity around an unmoving center, so that your mind is clear and ready to direct its attention wherever it may be needed. 99

TAKUAN
ZEN MASTER

CHINESE PHILOSOPHER MENCIUS

Yoga

*H*ATHA YOGA IS *a very popular form of exercise that originates from India. The body is held in various traditional postures that stretch the ligaments, leading to flexibility and general well-being. In the West this has become an end in itself. In India, however, this is only a part of the spiritual path of yoga. Yoga is not seen as merely physical exercise, but as a mystical science of body and mind that leads to mystical union with God. There are many forms of yoga, of which Hatha Yoga is only one. It is concerned with purifying the body to make it a perfect temple of the spirit.*

A HINDU YOGI

"YOGA" MEANS "UNION"

Hatha Yoga involves complex stretching exercises. It also works with the power of the breath and the mind to bring the yogi (practitioner) into harmony with the universe. The word "hatha" means "sun and moon." The word "yoga" means "union." The "sun and moon" represent the two great polarities of life, which the yogi seeks to unite in order to experience the transcendental Oneness.

each chakra and stimulating ever higher mystical states of consciousness. When it reaches the last and highest chakra, known as the "sahasrara" chakra or "the thousand-petaled lotus," the yogi's awareness is completely freed from the limitations of time and space and he or she experiences supreme bliss.

THE UNION OF SUN AND MOON

THE CHAKRAS

Hatha Yoga not only affects the physical body, it also invigorates the energy body that surrounds it. This energy body contains seven power points called "chakras," which means "wheels." The chakras are spinning centers of energy forming a natural mystic ladder that the yogi climbs on the spiritual journey to enlightenment.

KUNDALINI

Yogis teach that yoga can awaken a spiritual energy called "kundalini," which lies asleep at the base of the spine like a coiled snake. As it awakens, this power rises up through the spinal cord, invigorating

Centers of Energy – The Seven Chakras

The physical postures of yoga, and their associated breath and mind control exercises, energize and balance the chakras. This not only leads to bodily health but also produces extraordinary spiritual states of consciousness.

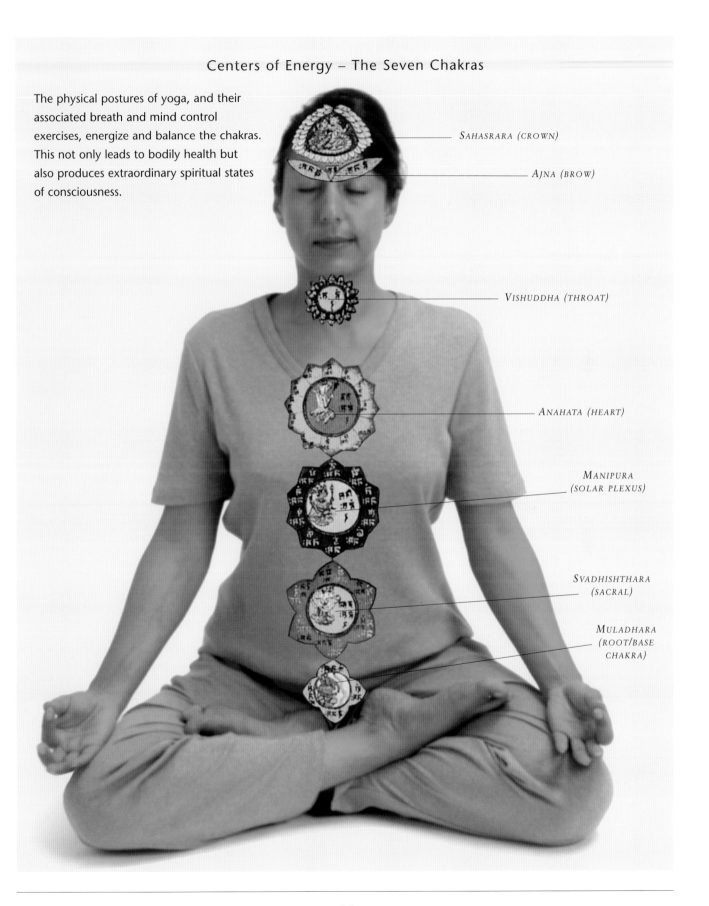

SAHASRARA (CROWN)

AJNA (BROW)

VISHUDDHA (THROAT)

ANAHATA (HEART)

MANIPURA (SOLAR PLEXUS)

SVADHISHTHARA (SACRAL)

MULADHARA (ROOT/BASE CHAKRA)

SALUTE TO THE SUN

The Hatha Yoga exercise "Soorya Namaskar" is better known as "Salute to the Sun." It is traditionally performed each morning facing the rising sun, which is regarded as the deity of health and long life. This exercise reduces abdominal fat, increases the breathing capacity, and brings flexibility to the spine and other limbs. It consists of 12 different positions, each of which stretches different ligaments.

1 Facing the sun, stand erect with hands held together in praying position with legs together.

2 Inhale, stretch the arms up over your head, and bend backward.

3 Exhale and bend forward until the hands are resting on the floor either side of the feet, with your head touching your knees. Beginners may bend the knees slightly so that the head can touch them.

4 Inhale and take a step backward with the right leg, keeping the hands and left foot firmly on the ground and the left knee between the hands. Bend the head backward.

5 Inhale and hold the breath. Move the left leg so that it is alongside the right leg, placing both feet together with the knees off the floor. Rest the weight on the hands with arms straight and keep the body in a straight line from head to feet.

6 Exhale and lower the body to the floor. This position is known as "sastanga

STEP 3

namaskar" or "eight-curved prostration" because eight parts of the body are in contact with the floor: forehead, chest, two hands, two knees, and two feet. If possible, the nose and abdominal region are slightly lifted.

7 Inhale and bend backward, with hips on the ground and bending the spine as much as possible.

STEP 4

8 Exhale and lift the body, keeping only the feet and hands flat on the floor.

9 Inhale and bring the right foot alongside the hands, with the left foot and knee touching the ground. Look upward. This is the same as position 4, except with the right foot forward rather than the left foot.

STEP 1

STEP 2

STEP 5

STEP 6

10 Exhale and bring the left foot up to the right foot, straighten the legs and bring the head down to the knees. This is the same as position 3 and once again beginners may bend the knees slightly so that the head can touch them.

11 Inhale as you raise the arms overhead and bend backward, stretching the spine. This is the same as position 2.

12 Exhale, straighten up, drop the arms, and relax for a few moments before repeating the exercise. It should be performed 12 times.

STEP 7

STEP 8

66 The body, being the temple of the living spirit, should be carefully tended in order to make it a perfect instrument. 99

SWAMI VISHNU-DEVANANDA
YOGA MASTER

❦❦❦❦

66 Purity of the mind is not possible without purity of the body in which it functions, and by which it is affected. 99

SWAMI VISHNU-DEVANANDA

❦❦❦❦

66 To identify consciousness with that which merely reflects consciousness – this is egoism. 99

YOGA APHORISMS
PATANJALI

❦❦❦❦

66 The Atman – the experiencer – is pure Consciousness. It appears to be the ever-changing moods of the mind. But in reality it is the unchangeable. 99

YOGA APHORISMS
PATANJALI

Sacred sensuality

BECAUSE THE WEST *has been dominated by Christianity, which has often portrayed sensuality and sexuality as the work of the devil, it is sometimes supposed that spirituality is opposed to the enjoyment of the senses. In fact, there are many spiritual traditions that actively encourage us to delight in the body and all the pleasures it brings. The body is a regarded as a temple of the soul, to be honored as a great gift.*

COME TO YOUR SENSES

Many spiritual rituals, and the setting in which they are performed, are designed quite literally to "bring us to our senses." Temples and churches are magnificent structures deliberately fashioned to fill us with awe. They are often filled with vibrant paintings and golden statues that thrill the eye. Beautiful music and evocative incense are commonly used to give us a taste of heaven on earth.

SACRED SEXUALITY

In India there are massive temple complexes decorated from top to bottom with representations of couples performing every imaginable sexual act. This is not pornography but reflects the idea of sexual love as a form of worship. Many spiritual rituals find their roots in ancient fertility rites, so it is not surprising that representations of erect phalluses are some of the most ancient sacred objects. Stone representations of the god Shiva's phallus, called Shiva lingams, are found throughout India. Statues of the god Amon with an erect phallus were, likewise, common in ancient Egypt.

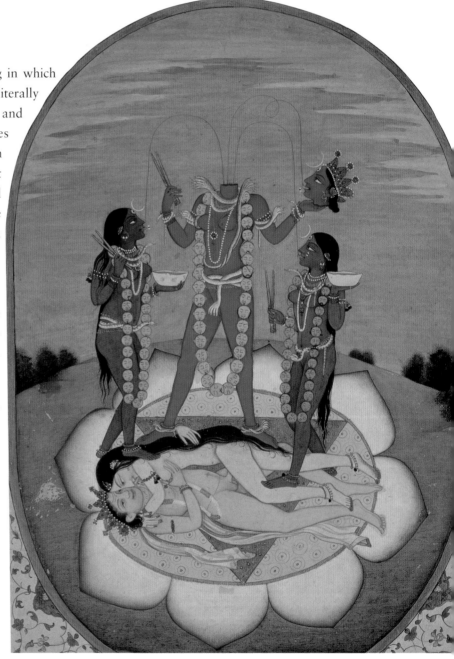

SPIRITUALITY THROUGH SEXUALITY

TANTRIC SPIRITUAL TRADITION

The Tantric spiritual tradition includes forms of yoga that use sexuality as a way of communing with God. Tantra began about 5000 BCE in India as a cult of the god Shiva and his consort Shakti. According to myth, as a result of their loveplay, Shakti gave form to Shiva's spirit and the universe was created. Sexuality is an opportunity to partake in the divine union of Shiva and Shakti. Couples practicing Tantra sometimes visualize themselves as the god and goddess while they are making love, to heighten their spiritual awareness.

Zorba the Buddha

The rascal guru Bagwan Shree Rajneesh offered the imaginary figure of "Zorba the Buddha" as the ideal human being – a combination of the transcendental insight of Buddha with the sensual passion of Zorba the Greek. The modern Indian sage Ramesh Balsekar explains that an enlightened being is a "super-bhoghi" – a "super-enjoyer." This is because the enlightened one is unattached and allow things to come and go as life dictates. He or she is, therefore, able to relish the delights of the moment without suffering because of the knowledge that they will inevitably pass. Only in this way can life be fully appreciated.

66 Here in the body are the sacred rivers, here are the sun and moon, as well as the pilgrimage places. I have not encountered another temple as blissful as my own body. 99

SARAHA DOHA
HINDU SAGE

66 To follow the Way do not push away anything – even sensual experiences and thoughts. In fact, to accept them completely is enlightenment. 99

SENG-T'SAN
ZEN MASTER

A LUXURIOUS BATH

Spirituality isn't all about asceticism and being "holy." It's about enjoying being alive. Sensual enjoyment is a great blessing to be celebrated. So, instead of performing some "pious" spiritual practice, prepare yourself a luxurious bath and meditate on the pleasure of relaxing in warm water.

- *Use essential oils.*
- *Light some candles and burn some incense.*
- *Play some gentle music.*
- *Be good to yourself!*

TAKE TIME TO ENJOY SENSUAL PLEASURES

Ritual

MOST SPIRITUAL TRADITIONS *utilize the power of ritual. Rituals are physical acts that symbolically represent spiritual events. In the ritual of the Eucharist, for example, by eating bread and drinking wine, symbolizing the body and blood of Christ, Christians commune with God. The intention of performing the ritual act is to actualize the spiritual event it represents. Through symbolically communing with God, actual commune may take place.*

GOD AS CHRIST

SACRED THEATER

During rituals, candles are often burned and the air is filled with incense and song, special words are spoken, and symbolic dress is worn – all of which increase the magic of the occasion and help bring about an altered state of awareness in the participants. In many ways ritual resembles theater, which is not surprising because the first playwrights, such as Sophocles and Euripides, based their tragedies on ancient rituals that dramatized Pagan myths. Participants in ritual, however, are not just passive spectators. They actively engage with the process and so experience spiritual purification, which the ancient Greeks called "catharsis."

EMPTY FORMALITY

The danger with ritual is that over time it degenerates into an empty formality without any real spiritual power. Ritual is not an end in itself to be "religiously" performed. It is a means to spiritual transformation. As the Hindu sage Sankara puts it:

"Observe ceremonies, sing devotional hymns, and worship as many gods as you please, but liberation will never come, even after a hundred eons, without realizing the Oneness."

❝ It is right that religious ceremonies be performed, but they bear little fruit compared to the ceremony of following the Buddha's teachings. ❞

KING ASOKA
BUDDHIST SAGE

CHRISTMAS CANDLES
IN UKRAINE

A FIRE CEREMONY

If you want to experience the power of ritual you may like to take part in a Native American Sweat Lodge ceremony, or a Buddhist Puja ritual, or attend a Sunday Eucharist at your local church. You will often find such events being advertised in your local bookstore.

If organized events do not appeal to you, it is easy to run your own ceremony, either alone or with a group of spiritual friends. A simple ritual to perform is a fire ceremony to purge unwanted ways of being.

1 *Build a fire, ideally outdoors, and gather around it in quiet meditation.*

2 *Write down on pieces of paper those habitual ways of being that you are now ready to let go of – such as anger, jealousy, or impatience, for example.*

3 *Offer up a prayer and throw your pieces of paper into the flames where your habit will be symbolically consumed, leaving you free to live in new and creative ways.*

I want to get rid of my fear of saying what I really feel

i've had enough of being a jealo person

I am ready to let go of needing to see myself as better than other people

Devotion

*D*EVOTION IS A PATH *of the heart. It is not concerned with things making sense to the intellect, but with entering a passionate love affair with Life. Devotees sing hymns, repeat liturgy, chant scriptures, bow before icons, perform rituals, and offer prayers – all of which invoke ecstatic states of joy and rapture. As the Hindu sage Ramakrishna explains, the intent of the spiritual philosopher is to become God, but the spiritual devotee wants to "taste the sweetness, not be the sugar." Devotees lose themselves in their longing for God and in so doing taste God's sweet love. As the Hindu saint Anandamayi Ma teaches, "The intense desire for God is itself the way to God."*

REJOICING

A PERSONAL GOD

Devotees give the ineffable Oneness a human face so they can relate emotionally to what may otherwise seem merely an abstract philosophical principle. Ramakrishna explains:

"Imagine God as a sea without shores. Through the cooling love of the devotee some of the water becomes frozen into blocks of ice. Now and then, God assumes a form and reveals Himself to his lovers as a Person. But when the sun of Knowledge rises, the blocks of ice melt away and God is without form, no more a Person. He is beyond description. Who could describe Him? Anyone who tries disappears, unable to find his 'I' anymore."

FALLING IN LOVE WITH LOVE

The Higher Power may appear to devotees as a mighty king before whom they should bow in humility, or as a loving father, or as an intimate friend or lover. From a spiritual point of view it is not important what form devotion takes, only the sincerity of the devotee, for this alone will genuinely open the heart to God. Practiced with sincerity, devotion purifies the consciousness of everything but God, until the devotee's individual identity dissolves into the Beloved. If this goal is not kept clearly in mind, devotion can become an empty religious formality. Then, as the Sufi sage Rumi teaches, devotion is not praise, but "proof of separation."

A STUDENT MEDITATES WITH THE GURU

Hindu or Christian?

Although different religions regard themselves as implacably opposed, if they just concentrated on their shared devotion to the Higher Power there would be no conflict. The following are two similar teachings concerning the power of devotion to bring the devotee into communion with God. One is from the Srimad Bhagavatam, a Hindu scripture. The other is from Diadochos of Photiki, a Christian saint. Can you tell which is which?

PASSAGE ONE

"Those who consciously love God in their hearts never lose an intense longing for spiritual illumination, until they feel it in their bones and no longer know themselves but are completely transformed by the love of God. They are both present in this life and not present. They live in the body, but have departed from it, as through love they ceaselessly journey in their souls toward God. Their hearts constantly burn with the fire of love and they cling to God with an irresistible fervor, for they have, once and for all, transcended self-love in their love for God."

PASSAGE TWO

"He who loves God is made pure; his heart melts in joy. He rises to transcendental consciousness by the rousing of his higher emotional nature. Tears of joy flow from his eyes, his hair stands on end, his heart melts in love. The bliss in that state is so intense that, forgetful of himself and his surroundings, he sometimes weeps profusely, or laughs, or sings, or dances; such a devotee is a purifying influence upon the whole universe."

ANSWER
The first passage is Christian and the second is Hindu.

HINDU GOD SHIVA WITH FEMALE DEVOTEES

A CHRISTIAN PRAYER BOOK AND ROSARY

Sacred Love Songs

Many of the great mystics, such as the Hindu Mirabai and the Christian John of the Cross, expressed their holy longing for God in sublime devotional poems of fervent passion and poignant yearning:

"Dark One, hear me, I am mad with visions.
Eaten up by separation,
*   I wander from place to place*
*   covered in ash and clothed in skins.*
My body is wasting all because of you.
Distraught and desperate,
I go from forest to forest.
Immortal and Unborn One, visit your beggar.
Extinguish her pain with your pleasurable touch.
Mirabai says: 'End this coming and going
Let me forever embrace your sweet feet.'"

MIRABAI
HINDU MYSTIC

"My Beloved is the high mountains,
and the lonely valley forests;
unexplored islands, rushing rivers,
and the love songs of the wind;
the hushed night-time and the waking dawn;
the soundless music of silent solitude;
the supper that nourishes
*   and swells me with love."*

ST. JOHN OF THE CROSS
CHRISTIAN MYSTIC

A TASTE OF SWEET DEVOTION

A simple way of experiencing the sweetness of devotion is to start your other regular spiritual practices, such as meditation, with a short devotional ritual.

1 *Find a devotional song or poem that touches your heart, or compose your own mystical poem that captures your heartfelt longing for divine communion.*

2 *Recite or sing your devotional offering to the Higher Power over and over again with increasing intensity. At the same time you may like to bow your head before some symbol that represents the object of your veneration.*

3 *Reach out with your heart and pour all your love into your devotional practice. If you are going to follow the path of devotion you will need to be able to abandon self-consciousness! Such devotional outpourings can be wonderfully powerful when alone in nature, addressed to the rising sun or the moon and shining stars.*

Let me dissolve my grateful heart in your bounty.

This longing echoes around my hollow heart – "inhabit me again!"

You are the ground on which I walk.

You are the silence in which I talk.

" Filth on hands, feet, and body
may be washed off with water;
Clothes fouled by dirt may be washed with soap;
The mind fouled by sin and evil
may only be cleansed by devotion to God. "

ADI GRANTH
SIKH SCRIPTURE

❀❀❀❀

" Between Almighty God and a devoted soul pass
many spiritual visits, sweet inward conversations,
great gifts of grace, many consolations,
much heavenly peace, and wonderful intimacy
with the blessed Presence. "

THOMAS A KEMPIS
CHRISTIAN SAGE

❀❀❀❀

" Blessed is the person whose desire for God has
become like the lover's passion for the beloved. "

JOHN CLIMACUS
CHRISTIAN SAGE

❀❀❀❀

" When you strip off your self-image,
There is no devotion or devotee.
Lover and Beloved are united,
In the light of your eyes. "

JOHN CLIMACUS
CHRISTIAN SAGE

Honoring the gods

TO LIVE HAPPY, FULFILLING LIVES *we have to be able to juggle all of life's many competing demands. We need to take care of our homes, but not at the expense of the wider community; to devote ourselves to spirituality, but not at the expense of practicality. If we ignore any important aspect of life we will be courting disaster. Polytheistic spiritual traditions help us remember this fundamental truth by teaching that we must honor all of the gods and goddesses who preside over different parts of life, for if we do not we will incur the wrath of some jealous unpropitiated deity.*

LIVE A BALANCED LIFE

ANCIENT POLYTHEISM AND MODERN PSYCHOLOGY

Modern psychology has adapted some of the teachings of Polytheism into a completely contemporary context. Freud and Jung, the founding fathers of psychoanalysis, studied the dreams of their patients and found that the ancient deities and their myths were still alive in the hidden recesses of the unconscious mind. Transposed into a modern psychological context, Polytheism can teach us how to live fulfilled and fortunate lives, in much the same way that it did our ancient ancestors.

66 Prayers serve to enhance the general reverence for God and create a sacred, indissoluble bond of fellowship with the gods. 99

IAMBLICHUS
PAGAN SAGE

SIGMUND FREUD

SUBPERSONALITIES

The self can be viewed as being made up of various competing personalities, which are comparable to the feuding gods and goddesses of myth, united by an impersonal and ineffable "I am," which corresponds to the supreme One God. Like the gods and goddesses, our various subpersonalities all demand to be honored. If we overly serve one, we may well have to face the displeasure of another, which can lead to anything from confusion to serious psychological problems. Through honoring all the aspects of ourselves – the gods and goddesses within – we can come into a unified state where every part has its place within the harmonious whole.

66 May all the gods grant me peace! 99

ATHARVA VEDA
HINDU SCRIPTURE

HONORING THE GODS WITHIN

This exercise can help you harmonize the needs of your various subpersonalities, so that no aspect of your character feels suppressed and rejected.

1 Examine yourself and become aware of some of your subpersonalities. There may be a part of you that feels it must achieve something important, or a part that just wants to enjoy sensual pleasures, or a part that craves attention from others, or a part that wants to be an isolated hermit. Whatever the characteristics of your particular sub-personalities, become as clear about them as you can. You may like to even give them each a name.

2 Imagine your sub-personalities to be like powerful but capricious deities. Respectfully ask each of them what it wants of you and whether it feels appropriately honored at the moment.

3 You might find, for example, that your sensual-self is angry that you have spent so much time lately honoring your achieving-self that you have found no time to enjoy a long hot bath. Your hermit-self might feel so ignored that, if you don't make some space to be on your own soon, he will make you ill and force you into a period of reclusive introspection.

4 Having understood what these different "gods within" require of you, negotiate with them to come up with ways to honor all of them. You may promise your sensual-self a weekend at a health farm or your hermit-self a week of meditative retreat, while explaining to your achieving-self that this does not mean that you are being irresponsible and ceasing to honor the god of work. The important thing is to not leave any powerful unhonored gods angrily pacing the underworld of your unconscious, plotting against you!

CONCENTRATE ON EVERY
ASPECT OF YOUR LIFE

Purification

MANY SPIRITUAL PRACTICES *are designed to purify the body and mind, and so encourage spiritual states of awareness. Practicing physical disciplines, such as refraining from eating meat or fasting completely, are ways of purifying the body. In the spring month of Ramadan, Muslims fast from dawn till dusk; Christians also fast during the period of Lent. Becoming permanently or temporarily celibate is also a common method of purification, used to tame the desires of the flesh. Meditation and taking a vow of silence are examples of methods used to purify the mind.*

CALL TO PRAYER

ASCETICISM

Certain sects in all religions have adopted ascetic practices to become full of spirit by completely purifying themselves of the world altogether. Francis, the 13th-century Christian saint, rejected all worldly comforts and "wedded" himself to "lady Poverty." Mahvira (b. 540,) the founder of Jainism, is one among many Eastern ascetics. For 13 years he wore only a simple loin cloth. Eventually, discarding this as well, he went around naked for the rest of his life. He attained enlightenment at the end of a long fast. The Buddha grew up a privileged aristocrat but became a rigorous ascetic for many years, before finally finding a "middle way" between austerities and indulgences.

FOLLOW YOUR OWN NATURE

Some spiritual masters, such as the early Gnostic Christian sages, teach that spiritual seekers should simply follow their own natures. If they want to be ascetics – that is God's will. If they prefer to indulge themselves and be promiscuous – that is also God's will. All that matters is the sincerity of the seeker's desire to awaken spiritually.

ST. FRANCIS

Baptism

Sometimes purification is achieved symbolically through ritual. Baptism, for example, is a central ceremony of Christianity that originally entailed complete submersion in water from which the initiate emerged purified and spiritually reborn. This ritual was previously practiced in the Pagan Mystery religion in which initiates would purify themselves by bathing in the ocean. In India today millions, likewise, regularly bathe in the holy Ganges River to purify themselves.

The Final Stage of Life

A Hindu scripture called the Laws of Manu teaches that at the end of a full family life spiritual seekers should abandon all their worldly responsibilities, purifying themselves in preparation for death by adopting an austere solitary life of spiritual detachment. In this way they may use the last years of life to attain "moksha" or spiritual liberation.

Missing the Point

Four Zen pupils had promised to observe a rule of silence for seven days. On the first day all were silent, but when night came the oil lamps began burning dimly and one of the pupils could not help exclaiming, "Someone should fix those lamps." The second pupil was shocked to hear him speak and cautioned him, "We are not supposed to say a word." "You idiots," said the third, "Now you've both spoken." "I am the only one who has not talked," proclaimed the fourth.

ZEN TEACHING STORY

THE SWEAT LODGE

Various forms of sweat lodges have been used from very early times throughout the world as a means of purification. Unlike the sauna at the local gym today, these ceremonial lodges are sacred places and taking part in a sweat is a profoundly spiritual experience.

The most famous sweat lodges are those of the Native Americans, traditionally small temporary erections made of willow poles covered with buffalo hides or birch bark. In these dark enclosures hot stones are covered with water, creating a steam bath that cleanses and invigorates the body. While this is happening, participants sing sacred songs and offer up prayers so that the process also purifies the soul. The sweat lodge is a ritual womb from which the participants emerge spiritually reborn.

A SWEAT LODGE IS A PLACE OF PHYSICAL AND SPIRITUAL CLEANSING

Every element in the construction of a sweat lodge and of the sweat ritual has symbolic spiritual significance. The stones, for example, represent the element of earth. The heat they carry represents fire. The steam represents air. The water poured on the stones and the sweat of the participants represents water.

Such forms of ceremonial purification are ubiquitous. Steam purification is widely practiced in Africa. The ancient Japanese had ceremonial steam baths called mushi-buro. The ancient Celts constructed sweat lodges of earth and stone. In northern Russia they constructed them of wood, sometimes partially submerged in the ground, or even totally underground. The polar Inuit, also known as Eskimos, even practice ceremonial sweats inside their igloos.

NATIVE AMERICANS USE SWEAT LODGES TO PURIFY THE SOUL BEFORE SACRED RITUALS

FASTING

Fasting is a traditional spiritual practice that purifies the body and strengthens the mind by requiring you to resist the overwhelming compulsion to eat.

To begin with it is best to fast only for a day, but when you are an experienced faster you may extend this for a number of days.

Initially you may want to limit yourself to a day eating just fruit or drinking only fruit juice. When fasting for a number of days, you may start and end your fast with a day on juices.

While fasting, you will probably feel lethargic and may get a headache as your body clears itself of toxins. But afterward you should feel refreshed and invigorated.

Many people find it helpful to fast regularly one day each week.

LIMIT YOURSELF TO FRUIT AND FRUIT JUICES WHEN FASTING

A VOW OF SILENCE

Taking a vow of silence is like fasting for the mind. Select a day when you will not need to communicate with others very much. Decide that you will not speak for a certain number of hours or even the whole day.

You many need to carry a little notebook with you to write down anything you cannot avoid communicating to others, but ideally try to be alone.

Being silent can be an extraordinary experience of peace that helps you to also still the inner chatter of the mind.

66 What is purity? Thinking only holy thoughts. 99

MOTTO OF THE PAGAN HEALING
SANCTUARY OF ASCLEPIUS

❃❃❃❃

66 In the sauna one must conduct oneself as if one were in church. 99

TRADITIONAL FINNISH SAYING

❃❃❃❃

66 He who uses silence in lieu of speech really does speak. 99

LIEH TZU
TAOIST SAGE

Repentance

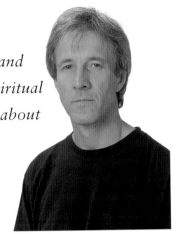

THE SAINTS AND SAGES *teach us to examine ourselves regularly and repent of our shortcomings, as a necessary step on the path of spiritual transformation. Repentance is not about seeing how bad we are. It is about clearing away the past so that we are constantly free to begin afresh. If we do not, we will inevitably repeat our errors until they are an ingrained aspect of our personality, preventing further spiritual awakening. By consciously feeling shame for our mistakes, we prevent the cancer of guilt.*

SOUL-SEARCHING

PUBLIC CONFESSION

Many spiritual traditions utilize the power of confession. Some schools of Taoism required public confession of all misdeeds as a prelude to spiritual rebirth. A public confession was also required of initiates into the ancient Pagan Mystery religion before candidates could undergo secret spiritual initiation. This was no empty formality, but was treated as a truly sacred act in which all must be openly and honestly revealed. The despotic Roman emperor Nero turned back from seeking initiation into the Greek Mysteries when he realized he would have to confess publicly to having murdered his mother. Not even a tyrant could face lying before the most sacred institution of the ancient world.

PRIVATE CONFESSION

Other traditions encourage a more private confession. Catholicism requires regular confession of all sins to a priest before partaking of the Eucharist. Other traditions teach us to offer our repentance personally before God or our own conscience. The ancient Pagan philosopher Seneca reports:

"Every day I plead my case before myself. When the light is extinguished, I examine the past day, go over and weigh all my deeds and words. I hide nothing, I omit nothing: why should I hesitate to face my shortcomings when I can say to myself 'Take care not to repeat them' and also 'I forgive you today'?"

A CATHOLIC PRIEST HEARS CONFESSION

EACH NIGHT REVIEW THE DAY THAT HAS PASSED

REVIEW THE DAY

Every night before falling asleep, take a few moments to review your day and acknowledge your shortcomings. Forgive yourself and affirm your determination to awaken spiritually. Then step peacefully into the night world of dreams and the exquisite peace of deep sleep.

> 66 The sin that makes you sad and repentant is liked better by the Lord than the good deed that turns you vain and conceited. 99
>
> NAHJUL BALAGHA
> MUSLIM SCRIPTURE

I Can't Help It

When the Christian mystic Brother Lawrence became aware of his failings, he acknowledged them with a sincere sense of his own inadequacy. But he knew he could never prevent himself from messing up, so he simply surrendered the situation to God, praying, "If you leave me to myself, I cannot help but fall. It is You that must hinder my falling and put right what is amiss." After this he worried about the situation no further.

Service

SAINTS AND SAGES *from every spiritual tradition teach that selfless service is a better way to God than religious rituals or esoteric spiritual practices. The Sufi sage Sa'di explains, "The path is service of others, not prayer beads and Dervish robes." Judaism teaches, "He who does not perform deeds of loving kindness is as one who has no God," for "deeds of kindness are equal in weight to all the commandments." When followers of the Hindu guru Neem Karoli Baba would ask him how they could achieve enlightenment he would simply reply, "Feed people."*

THE GOOD SAMARITAN

SERVING OTHERS IS SERVING GOD

Christianity teaches "It is more blessed to give than to receive." In the Gnostic Gospel of Thomas, Jesus advises, "If you have money, do not lend it at interest, but give to one from whom you will not get it back." In the "Parable of the Sheep and Goats," he paints a picture of the Day of Judgment in which the Son of Man praises those who have served others and condemns those who have not. Jesus teaches that when we help the needy, we are helping God. If we do not, we are allowing God to suffer. God is in all of us. What we do to others, we do to God. Mother Theresa of Calcutta said that when caring for the dying and destitute she just saw "Christ in all his distressing disguises."

LOVE IN ACTION

As a spiritual practice, the value of service lies not just in what we do but also in why we do it. Judaism teaches, "The whole worth of a benevolent deed lies in the love that inspires it." To make service a spiritual practice that helps us transcend the ego-self, our actions must be more than doing what is expected of us or looking for social recognition, which only leads to self-aggrandizement. This is why Jesus advises, "When you give alms, do not let your left hand know what your right hand is doing." Spiritual service must be humble and anonymous love in action.

MOTHER THERESA

SERVICE IS NATURAL

The Hindu guru Sai Baba condenses his teachings to the slogan "Love all, serve all." When we serve all, we begin to love as God loves. Our service is not a moral requirement, but rather a spontaneous response to experiencing the suffering of others. If we see ourselves and others as expressions of the Oneness of God, service is as natural and unaffected as the right hand helping the left hand. The Buddhist sage Shantideva explains:

"When I work for the sake of others, I should not let conceit or the feeling that I am wonderful arise. It is just like feeding myself – hoping for nothing in return."

ENJOY PROVIDING FOR OTHERS

Selfless Service

The Taoist sage Lao Tzu teaches, "When being of service or caring for others, let go of your ideas about how it should be." If we are attached to our actions producing the results we believe are desirable, no matter how seemingly altruistic, we will be expressing our own will not offering up our service to the Higher Power and accepting the will of Life. A Hindu scripture called the Bhagavad Gita teaches that for our service to help us achieve selflessness, we must be completely unattached to the fruits of our actions. More than this, it teaches that service is only truly selfless when we have no sense of being the "doer," but rather of God acting through us. Service is being a willing vehicle through which that great Love that is the Higher Power naturally expresses itself.

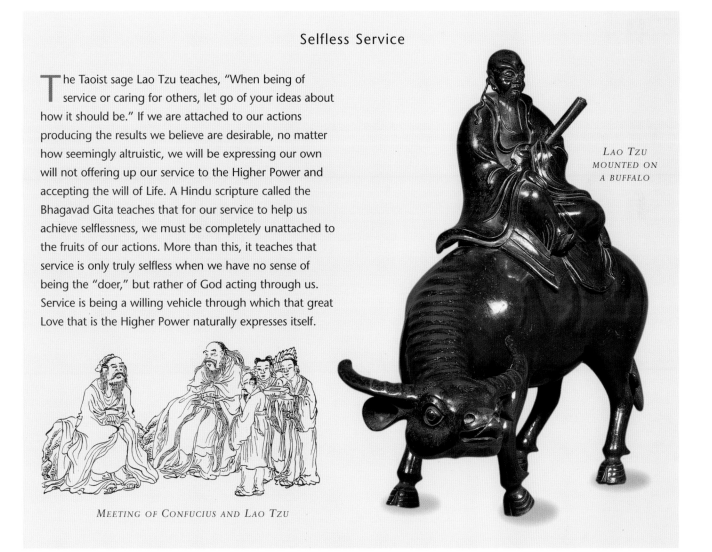

LAO TZU
MOUNTED ON
A BUFFALO

MEETING OF CONFUCIUS AND LAO TZU

Natural Goodness

The Taoist sage Lao Tzu teaches that true service is not about trying to appear to be a "do-gooder," but spontaneously and effortlessly expressing our innate Natural Goodness. He writes:

"A do-gooder wants to be seen to be good.
Natural Goodness is unconcerned with appearances.
A do-gooder may be endlessly busy,
but there always seems more to be done.
Natural Goodness seems to do nothing
and good things just happen.

Natural Goodness is like a deep well inside of you.
If you have been drawing from this well,
then nothing is impossible.
There are no limits to what you can achieve,
and you are able to truly help."

MUSICIANS GAVE THEIR TIME AND TALENT TO RAISE MONEY FOR LIVE AID

HELPING OUT

A good way to experience the power of service is to do some voluntary work with a local charity. Choose an area where there is a particular need that you are aware of and you feel you have something to contribute. You don't need to do something with an organization to be of service, however. The world is full of opportunities to help others who are less fortunate than ourselves and experience the joys of service.

To make service a spiritual practice you should be conscious of your inner attitude. Concentrate on breaking down any barriers created by the roles of "helper" and "helped." Make sure you see those you are assisting as other human beings just like you, not the "needy" or "helpless."

Allow natural compassion to flow through you. If helping is an effort, it isn't service. Become a willing vehicle for the compassion of the Higher Power.

Although for you service is a spiritual practice, be careful not to lay a "spiritual trip" on those you are helping. Those who use service as a means of spreading their own beliefs or recruiting members to their particular spiritual club are evangelizing, not practicing selfless service.

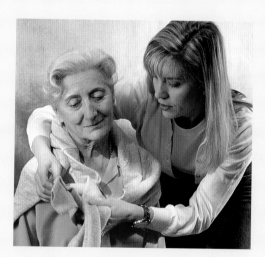

OFFER HELP WITHOUT EXPECTATIONS

❝ Strive constantly to serve the welfare of the world. By devotion to selfless work one attains the supreme goal of life. Do your work with the welfare of others always in mind. ❞

KRISHNA IN THE BHAGAVAD GITA
HINDU SCRIPTURE

❝ When a person loses himself into God, he immediately finds himself in the service of all that lives. It becomes his delight and recreation. He is a new person never weary in the service of God's creation. ❞

MAHATMA GANDHI
HINDU SAGE

❝ Others are my main concern. When I notice something of mine, I steal it and give it to others. ❞

SHANTIDEVA
BUDDHIST SAGE

❝ Even three times a day to offer three hundred cooking pots of food does not match a portion of the merit acquired in one instant of love. ❞

NAGARJUNA
BUDDHIST SAGE

Pilgrimage

FOR CENTURIES SPIRITUAL SEEKERS *have set off on holy pilgrimages. Whether through historical coincidence or divine dispensation, certain places have become centers of spiritual energy, and making a journey to such sacred sites can be powerfully transformative. Christians journey to the Holy Land. Buddhists travel to the places where the Buddha preached. Shamans head out into the wilderness. Muslims are expected to make a pilgrimage to the Kaaba in Mecca at least once during a lifetime, if at all possible.*

MUSLIMS PRAYING AT MECCA

A PHYSICAL ENACTMENT OF THE INNER JOURNEY

A pilgrimage is a spiritual practice not a vacation. It is a physical enactment of the inner journey to God, during which pilgrims concentrate their minds in meditation and prayer, and open their hearts with devotional worship. Some pilgrims make the journey a form of ascetic practice, deliberately taking the most arduous route or walking when other transportation is available. Some pilgrims even crawl or progress through a sequence of full-length prostrations.

Some Things You Must Do Yourself

T'ao-ch'ein asked a fellow monk to accompany him on a pilgrimage to assist him in his practice of Zen. His friend said, "I'll certainly try to help you in any way I can, but there are some things you must do yourself." "What do you mean?" asked T'ao-ch'ein. His friend replied, "Well, my eating or drinking will not fill your stomach. When you want to urinate, there's nothing I can do about it. And only you can make your body walk along the road." This answer opened T'ao-ch'ein's mind and he made the journey alone.

ZEN TEACHING STORY

PILGRIMS AT KEDARNATH, A SOURCE OF THE GANGES RIVER

MAKING A PILGRIMAGE

To make a spiritual pilgrimage you do not need to be part of an organized religion. Think of some special place that has spiritual meaning for you. Perhaps a local hill that you can walk to, or an ancient sacred site that you will need to drive to, or even a holy place in a distant land. It doesn't matter how you get there, only that it requires some effort and determination on your part and that you make it a spiritual journey, not simply a day out or a week off.

You can travel with other spiritual pilgrims, or you may prefer to journey on your own so that you can stay focused on your pilgrimage as a spiritual practice.

The point of the pilgrimage is what you learn on the journey, not just arriving at the place you have chosen. Be aware of your inner world and your spiritual destination as you travel through the outer world to your physical destination.

If your pilgrimage takes place over many days, it is a good idea to keep a spiritual diary of your thoughts and feelings, and the adventures that happen to you on the way.

MAKE NOTES IN A SPIRITUAL DIARY

A TIBETAN BUDDHIST AT ULAANBAATAR IN MONGOLIA

66 Do you want to be a pilgrim on the path of Love? The first step is making yourself humble as ashes. 99

ANSARI OF HERAT
SUFI SAGE

66 To stop simply hanging on to what has been in the past and longing for what might be in the future is better than making a ten-year pilgrimage. 99

LIN-CHI
ZEN MASTER

Spiritual retreat

*U**NDERTAKING A SPIRITUAL** retreat is a form of spiritual "hot-housing." It provides us with the opportunity to focus intensively on our spiritual practices, away from the distractions of everyday life. Deep spiritual transformation often involves periods of profound discomfort and disorientation that would be undesirable in the context of normal life. A place of retreat, such as a Christian monastery or Hindu ashram, is a safe space in which to undergo and move beyond such difficult phases of growth, giving us the chance to progress to a completely new level of spiritual understanding.*

MONASTIC COMMUNITIES

Some spiritual traditions encourage regular short retreats. Others require a long period of retreat of a year, or a number of years, to be made at some stage during a seeker's spiritual training. Some people choose to transform their whole lives into a spiritual retreat by becoming part of a monastic community or adopting the life of a solitary hermit. Most monastic communities require their members to be celibate, obey strict rules of conduct, partake in communal spiritual practice, share most property in common, adopt a simple uniform that marks them out as being a monk or nun, and work in the monastery to contribute toward the physical needs of the community. Some require members to take holy vows, promising to conform to the rules of the community for the rest of their lives.

FIRST-CLASS SEEKERS?

It is sometimes presumed that only those who adopt such a lifestyle are really taking spirituality seriously, while everyone else is a second-class seeker. But this is complete nonsense. Living a monastic life is full of as many spiritual dangers as opportunities, just like every other lifestyle. There is no doubt that monasteries and ashrams are powerful sources of spiritual inspiration, but living in one is a quite different experience from making an occasional visit. All the dramas of life that everyone experiences do not disappear. The monastery becomes a place of personal rivalries and intrigue just like any other human community.

Being a monk or nun can just be a way of becoming a special "spiritual person" rather than genuinely transcending the ego-self. Whether one becomes a permanent member of a spiritual community or not is simply a matter of finding the path that suits one's individual temperament. Spirituality teaches us to be completely natural, and for most of us the most natural way to live is in the world, working to feed ourselves, caring for our families, and contributing to our communities, as well as performing our inner spiritual work. In living such a life, however, spirituality can often become neglected Going on retreat is a powerful way to make sure we keep our spiritual lives vibrant and exciting.

Why Have You Come to This Monastery?

A student came to a monastery to seek the truth of Buddhism. "Why have you come to this monastery?" asked the master. "Why do you neglect your own precious treasure at home?" "What is my treasure?" asked the student. "The one who asks the question is the treasure," replied the master.

ZEN TEACHING STORY

Desert Hermits

A brother asked the Christian hermit Abba Peomen, "I have found a place in the desert where I can live undisturbed by others. Do you advise me to live there?" Abba Peomen replied, "The place for you, my son, is where you will not disturb anyone else."

Another brother asked Abba Peomen, "How should I behave in my desert cell?" Abba Peomen replied, "Wherever you live, live like a stranger and do not expect your words to have any influence, then you will be at peace."

THE MIRISAVATIYA DAGOBA, A BUDDHIST TEMPLE, LIES ACROSS A LAKE IN ANURADHAPURA, SRI LANKA

GOING ON RETREAT

There are many Christian Friaries, Buddhist monasteries, Hindu ashrams, and so forth that accept visitors wishing to undertake personal retreats. The advantage of staying at such places is that you can enjoy the spiritual ambience that imbues permanent places of retreat. You also have the inspiration of other spiritual people around you and can join in their regular spiritual practices and monastic routines.

If this is too much like organized religion for you, then it is easy to set up your own retreat. Rent a little country cottage for a week. If you can't afford to go away, just set aside a room in your own house that you can inhabit for a day or two. This is more difficult, however, because you will be surrounded by familiar things that can easily draw you into the habitual states of mind you are seeking to free yourself from. You will also need to be sure that you will not be disturbed.

If you are new to undertaking a retreat, it is usually best to decide in advance how you are going to use your time so that you don't simply "space out." Put aside regular times for practices such as meditation, study of spiritual texts, contemplation, walking, and so on. Don't be too demanding on yourself. If you find it easy to stay focused, you can avoid planning anything and respond intuitively to your inner promptings.

6.00 Wake up and perform "salute to the sun"
6.30 Early meditation
7.30 Breakfast
8.00 Contemplative walk
10.30 Yoga
11.00 Morning meditation
12.00 Light lunch
1.00 Time for reading
3.00 Afternoon yoga
3.30 Afternoon meditation
4.30 Tea
5.00 Make daily notes in spiritual diary
6.00 Rest and relaxation
9.00 Evening prayers

STRUCTURE YOUR DAYS

SET ASIDE TIME FOR MEDITATION

A NEW ENVIRONMENT GIVES YOU THE OPPORTUNITY TO DEVELOP A NEW STATE OF MIND

Being on retreat can be a great joy, but it can also be tough. You can never be sure what it will throw up for you. Patience and perseverance will be your greatest allies. Don't expect miracles and, who knows, they just might happen. Although undertaking any sort of spiritual retreat can be a challenging ordeal and requires serious commitment, when approached in the right way it becomes an exciting adventure into new spiritual depths.

When you return from your spiritual retreat you may well be in an altered state of consciousness. There is a danger that you will find ordinary life jarring and difficult to cope with, and will experience a dramatic comedown. To guard against this, allow a short period to integrate your new-found peace of mind gently into the rest of your life, rather than setting up an unhealthy dichotomy between the "spiritual you" and the "everyday you."

*GET AWAY FROM
THE CROWD*

❝ In the beginning of the spiritual life we should faithfully do our duty and deny ourselves, but after that comes unspeakable pleasures. ❞

BROTHER LAWRENCE
CHRISTIAN MYSTIC

❦❦❦❦

❝ The most important rule for monks
is 'Be continually aware.' ❞

ATISHA
BUDDHIST MONK

❦❦❦❦

❝ The true mystic is not a reclusive saint who avoids others. The true mystic lives alongside other people – coming and going, eating and sleeping, buying and selling, marrying and chatting – but not for a moment does he forget God. ❞

ABU SA'ID IBN ABI-L-KHAYR
SUFI SAGE

ST. FRANCIS

Communing with Nature

T*HE FIRST AND greatest of all spiritual teachers is Nature herself. We are a part of Nature and through communing with the natural world we can overcome our sense of separateness and awaken an awareness of the Whole. For shamanic cultures, all of Nature – the wind, rain, animals, birds, fishes, grass, and stones – can teach us something about ourselves and the mystery of existence. The awesome beauty of Nature bypasses the rational mind and directly touches the heart. Nature's rich sensuality overwhelms our cultural conditioning and puts us in touch with the primal Power of Life.*

ALL OF NATURE
CAN TEACH US

RETREATING TO THE WILDERNESS

Many traditions encourage us to spend time in the wilderness communing with Nature, away from the comforts and hassles of towns and cities. In the gospels, Jesus is portrayed as spending 40 days and 40 nights in the wilderness where he receives visions of the devil whose temptations he must overcome. Muhammad received visions of the angel Gabriel while in meditative retreat in a mountain cave. In the Native American tradition, men and women head out to the wilderness in search of visions. Australian Aborigines go "walkabout" in the outback to practice "Sky Gazing" – a natural form of meditation that involves staring at the sky until consciousness is experienced as no longer limited to the body but as permeating the whole cosmos.

A Songbird's Sermon

One day a Zen master was just about to give a sermon when a bird started to sing. The master said nothing and everyone listened to the bird. When the song stopped, the master announced that the sermon had been preached and went on his way.

ZEN TEACHING STORY

AN AWE-INSPIRING WATERFALL IN OREGON

In Praise of Nature

I am the wind that breathes upon the sea,

I am the wave on the ocean,

I am the murmur of leaves rustling,

I am the rays of the sun,

I am the beam of the moon and stars,

I am the power of trees growing,

I am the bud breaking into blossom,

I am the movement of the salmon swimming,

I am the courage of the wild boar fighting,

I am the speed of the stag running,

I am the strength of the ox pulling the plow,

I am the size of the mighty oak,

And I am the thoughts of all people,

Who praise my beauty and grace.

THE BLACK BOOK OF CARMARTHEN
CELTIC CHRISTIAN SCRIPTURE

The mountains are a joyous place

full of flowers.

Monkeys play in the forest trees.

Songbirds sing and insects swarm.

A rainbow shines both day and night.

Summer and winter bring soothing rain.

Spring and autumn bring shifting fog.

Solitary, in simple clothes, I am happy here

because I see the Clear Light

and contemplate the emptiness.

I am delighted by appearances

because my body is free from bad actions.

A strong mind wanders contentedly

and is naturally cheerful.

MILAREPA
TIBETAN BUDDHIST SAGE

*A SYMBOLIC LANDSCAPE FROM THE GITAGOVINDA, A
SANSKRIT TEXT ABOUT THE LOVE OF KRISHNA AND RADHA*

THE VISION QUEST

Simply meditating in a natural beauty spot can be a particularly uplifting experience. But if you are feeling more adventurous you may like to set off on a Vision Quest, like the Native Americans.

1 *Having prepared yourself through meditation and prayer, go alone into as wild a natural environment as you can find. Without an experienced guide, it is best not to stray too far from help and assistance in case you need it. If it is warm enough, take with you only a blanket, water, and, perhaps, some sacred tobacco to smoke.*

2 *Calling on all the powers of your intuition, choose your spot carefully. Draw yourself a sacred circle of about six feet (two meters) diameter in the earth, or mark it out with small stones. Commit yourself to remaining within this circle for the duration of your Vision Quest. It is a powerful practice not to let your gaze move from beyond the limits of your circle.*

3 *If you decide to stay out overnight, be prepared for a testing ordeal in which you will have to confront your fears, as well as experience the wonders of communing with Nature. Try not to sleep but to be alert at all times. Offer up prayers to Great Spirit and the spirits of Nature. Become completely aware of Nature all around you. As you do so, allow yourself to become a part of Nature. Be Nature witnessing itself.*

NATIVE AMERICAN SHAMANS TRADITIONALLY GO IN QUEST OF VISIONS WITH NOTHING BUT A BLANKET AND A SACRED PIPE

TAKE WATER, A BLANKET, AND TOBACCO

4 *Pay attention to every detail of your experience. Notice if you are joined by any animals, birds, or even insects. Ask yourself what they have come to teach you. You may experience visions or have a sense that Nature is talking to you, either directly or through an animal, a tree, the wind, the rain, the earth, the nature spirits, and so forth. Don't worry if you do not.*

Whatever your particular experience, going on a Vision Quest is a powerful spiritual practice from which you will undoubtedly return transformed.

66 Instead of seeing Nature, see out of the eyes of Nature. See the world out of the eyes of a trout or a tree. There is a kind of grief and melancholy in human beings because of their inability to do this. 99

MARTÍN PRECHTEL
MAYAN SHAMAN

66 One Nature pervades and circulates within all natures. 99

YUNG-CHIA TA-SHIH
ZEN MASTER

❧❧❧❧

66 Don't live by your own rules, but in harmony with Nature. 99

EPICTETUS
PAGAN SAGE

BECOME PART OF NATURE

Sacred plants

Plants and herbs *are used by shamans the world over for healing and magical purification. Many shamanic cultures also use plants with hallucinogenic properties to induce mystical visions. In Central America shamans eat peyote and smoke* Saliva divinorum. *In the Amazon they drink a tea produced from the ayahuasca vine. In Siberia they ingest the fly agaric mushroom. For shamans, power plants are gifts from the gods that give them entrance to the spirit world.*

CANNABIS PLANT

NATURAL PSYCHEDELICS

Using natural psychedelics is one of the earliest forms of spirituality. The majority of the verses of the ancient Hindu Vedas, the most ancient of all scriptures, sing the praises of "Soma" – a mysterious milky psychedelic brew, which many believe to have been prepared from the fly agaric mushroom or similar hallucinogen. Scholars have also speculated that fly agaric, or some other powerful psychedelic plant, was the basis of the "Haoma" used in ancient Persian rites, as well as the "nectar" or "ambrosia" used as a mystical intoxicant in the ancient Greek Mystery religion. The fly agaric mushroom, with its red cap and white spots, is the familiar pixie mushroom of children's stories. Such fairy tales are memories of ancient European use of fly agaric by Celtic shamans to induce visions of elemental nature spirits – the "faery folk."

*CELTIC SHAMANS
USED FLY AGARIC
MUSHROOMS*

CANNABIS

Cannabis has been a popular sacred intoxicant from ancient times and remains so today. The Pagan priestess of the Oracle at Delphi in ancient Greece used cannabis to enter into a trance from which she delivered the prophecies of the god Apollo. Such "stoned" oracles were even consulted on important political matters by eminent statesmen. In India the holy "saddhu," lost in some ecstatic vision clutching his cannabis "chillum" pipe, is a familiar figure. In the Jamaican religion called Rastafarianism cannabis is smoked as a form of worship.

RASTAFARIANS SEE SMOKING AS A SPIRITUAL PRACTICE

Nature's Way

In the modern world, power plants are often lumped together with highly addictive synthesized drugs, such as heroin, and portrayed as destructive or even immoral. Many regard using any form of "drug" as an unnatural and unspiritual way of inducing altered states of awareness. Yet what could be more natural than eating a particular mushroom or smoking a certain herb and through the power of this magical plant communing with the spirits of Nature. Taking power plants can be psychologically demanding as well as physically unpleasant, involving nausea and vomiting, so it is not a recreational experience. Shamans regard power plants as spiritual teachers who offer a simple, organic way of transcending the limited horizons of the ego-self and experiencing a wider reality.

FLY AGARIC MUSHROOMS

Warning: *Fly agaric mushrooms can be extremely dangerous if they are not prepared in the right way. Do not attempt to pick and eat any of these mushrooms without seeking trustworthy advice.*

SHAMANIC RITUAL

Shamanic rituals involving power plants are best done by or under the supervision of an experienced shaman, but anyone can use sacred herbs to offer prayers to Great Spirit.

Sit by a small fire outside at night and quietly focus your mind in prayer. As you articulate your praise, gratitude, and petitions, throw a little of a sacred herb onto the fire to take your prayers up to Great Spirit. You can use any herb that you feel is appropriate. Sage is a good choice. As its name suggests, this herb is associated with wisdom and is universally recognized as having healing and purifying properties.

Tobacco is also a good choice of herb. It has received a bad name in the modern world through addictive overconsumption. Among the indigenous peoples of America, however, it is regarded as sacred. As well as offering tobacco into the flames, it can be smoked in a pipe. Honor the tobacco as a spirit guide. As you breathe out, imagine the smoke taking your prayers up to Great Spirit.

TOBACCO

For Native Americans, tobacco is the most sacred herb and the whole process of smoking is a spiritual practice. To be a pipe carrier is a responsibility and an honor, comparable to being a priest. The pipe's phallic-like stem symbolizes the male aspect of Great Spirit, and the bowl represents the female. Prayers are taken up to Great Spirit by the smoke as it rises into the air.

CHRISTIAN SHAMANISM

In America, Christianity has synthesized with indigenous Shamanism to produce some interesting spiritual hybrids. The Native American Church combines South American peyote Shamanism, indigenous North American spirituality, and European Christianity. The priest, known as a Road Man, leads the congregation in ingesting the powerful psychedelic power plant peyote. The Santo Daime Church is a Brazilian blend of Catholicism and Shamanism. As its eucharist it has the

AMAZONIAN SHAMANS SMOKING TOBACCO

"Daime" – a tea made from the Amazonian vine ayahuasca, which induces extraordinary visions. Both these religions are now legal, despite their use of psychedelics, and are seen by their practitioners as an authentic form of family worship. Aiko Aiyana, a member of the Santo Daime Church, explains:

"People want to call it a drug experience and I say, 'Well to us it's Holy Daime.' The Daime is a sacrament that I take that gets me there. It's like, I could walk somewhere for miles and it would take me some days. Or else I could jump on a jet and wow! I'm there straight away. And the Daime is like that. It's a true gift that I can use to heighten my level of awareness. The people who say 'It is just a drug' – I would invite them to drink the Daime and experience it for themselves."

A MEXICAN SUPPLIES PEYOTE, A HALLUCINATORY DRUG MADE FROM A CACTUS PLANT

A NATIVE AMERICAN PEACE PIPE

“ I have passed beyond sky and earth in my glory.

Have I been drinking Soma?

I will lift up the earth and put it here or there.

Have I been drinking Soma? ”

RIG VEDA
HINDU SCRIPTURE

❧❧❧❧

“ Ayahuasca makes one see and feel the spirits.
It teaches one about the true spiritual magic. ”

DON AUGUSTIN RIVAS VASQUEZ
SHAMAN

❧❧❧❧

“ Consider all the benefits that individuals and states in Greece have received from the Priestesses when they were intoxicated, although their usefulness in their sober senses amounts to little or nothing. ”

PLATO
PAGAN PHILOSOPHER

❧❧❧❧

“ Peyote is a medicine. On the reservation it is successfully used to cure alcoholism. Peyote stimulates visions. There are so many dimensions to everything and it sharpens you so you can read the messages right. ”

ERNESTO ALVARADO
APACHE SHAMAN

Music and dance

USIC AND DANCE *have always been used in spiritual rituals for their power to invoke altered states of awareness. Africans drum throughout the night until they are lost in the rhythm of life. Australian Aborigines induce trance with their bullroarers, click sticks, digeridoos, and rhythmical dancing. Tibetan Buddhists chant in voices so deep and resonant it is as if the bowels of the earth are issuing forth their vibrant mantras. The dignified harmonies of Christian Plainsong melt away the world and open up transcendental vistas of serenity.*

A TIBETAN MASTER

THE WHIRLING DERVISHES

The Whirling Dervishes, founded by the Sufi saint Rumi, induce rapture through swirling dances performed to the music of drums, flutes, and strings. They recite the name of Allah and dance ecstatically, with eyes closed, around a central master, known as a Shaikh. The Dervishes whirl both on their own axis and about the Shaikh, symbolizing the movement of the planets circling the sun. Eventually, consumed by euphoria, they collapse into the sublime stillness of union with God. In the Gnostic scripture called the Acts of John, Jesus similarly gathers his disciples around him in a circle and leads them in a sacred dance in which he sings and they all answer "amen."

THE SUN DANCE

Native Americans practice the Sun Dance. Having purified themselves in the Sweat Lodge and with fasting, the dancers ceremonially pierce their pectoral muscles with a cherrywood spike connected by a thong to the Sun Dance Tree at the center of the dancing circle. They then dance wildly without stopping for four days and four nights, blowing whistles made of eagle bones, which make the sound of the sacred eagle's cry. They must on no account fall, even when the cherrywood spike eventually rips through the skin of the chest. At dawn they greet the rising sun, singing:

> "Here am I – behold me.
> I am the sun – behold me."

WHIRLING DERVISHES

DANCING TO THE BEAT OF THE HEART

The indigenous peoples teach that the best place to experience the primal power of music and dance is out in Nature. With a group of spiritual friends, find a wild spot where you will not disturb anyone and build a fire. Gather around the fire in quiet prayer and feel the earth beneath you, the sky above you, and the spirits all around you.

1 *Having honored Great Spirit, begin to set up a simple rhythm using basic percussive instruments, such as drums, maracas, click sticks, and so on. Let the rhythm build as you pour your devotion into the music. Clap and sing – you don't necessarily need to use words.*

2 *Let the rhythm take control of your body. Sway and swirl. Don't try to control your movements but let them issue spontaneously from your deeper being. Abandon control and let the music and dance become an expression of the power of Nature that surrounds you.*

THE BEAUTY OF NATURE OPENS THE HEART

DANCING INDUCES TRANCE

66 The man made of wood starts to sing.
The woman made of stone starts to dance.
This cannot happen through learning or logic. 99

TUNG-SHAN
ZEN MASTER

❅❅❅❅

66 Around Him we dance the true dance;
God-inspired and no longer dissonant. 99

PLOTINUS
PAGAN SAGE

Magic

MAGIC IS BASED *on the ancient belief that the objective physical world and the subjective world of imagination are intimately connected. Magical practices are about using the inner power of the mind to bring about corresponding changes in the physical world. The controversial magician Aleister Crowley defined magic as "the science and art of causing change to occur in conformity with will." Whereas some forms of spirituality emphasize surrendering the will to God, magic is about using the will to control one's life.*

A SHAMAN'S RATTLE

JESUS THE MIRACLE WORKER

WHITE AND BLACK MAGIC

Magic can be divided into white magic and black magic. White magic is known as "the right-hand path," giving us the word "righteous." Black magic is known as "the left-hand path," giving us the word "sinister," which means "left." White magicians selflessly seek to serve others. Black magicians, on the other hand, use their powers to benefit their individual self-interest. Magic itself is neither bad nor good, it depends on the intent of the magician.

SPIRITUAL MAGICIANS

Many of the great masters are credited with magical powers. Ancient Pagan sages, such as Empedocles, were said to have foretold the future, cured sickness, stilled the wind, and raised the dead. The gospels attribute the same miracles to Jesus. In India, magical powers, known as "Siddhis," are well documented. They include being in two places at once, levitation, walking on water, reading minds, not needing to sleep, and surviving on nothing but air. The modern guru Sai Baba is famous for miraculously producing sacred ash from thin air. Most spiritual masters do not encourage their students to develop such magical powers, however, but to use them wisely should they spontaneously occur. It is more important to realize the miracle of ordinary life, which we usually completely overlook.

Knowledge without Wisdom

Jesus was walking in the desert with his followers who begged him to tell them the secret Name with which he raised the dead. Jesus replied, "If I tell you, you won't use it wisely." They continued, "We are ready master and it will strengthen our faith." "You don't know what you are asking," he told them. They insisted, however, so he revealed to them the Name. A little later, these people left Jesus and came upon a heap of whitened bones. "Let's try out that magic Name," one of them suggested – so they did. In an instant the bones became clothed with flesh and were transformed into a wild beast that tore them all to shreds. Such is the danger of knowledge without the wisdom to use it.

SUFI TEACHING STORY

66 Why is love called a Magician?

Because all the force of magic consists in love.

The parts of this world,

like the members of one animal,

depend all on one love

and are connected by natural communion.

Love is the common drawing together,

and this is the true magic. 99

MASILIO FICINO
RENAISSANCE MYSTIC

❊❊❊❊

66 Why! who makes much of a miracle?

As for me I know nothing but miracles. 99

WALT WHITMAN
MYSTICAL POET

THE MAGICAL IMAGINATION

Magic teaches that with our minds we create the world. A spiritual practice that applies this principle is to use the creative imagination to dream into being the future you.

1 *Sit in meditation and envisage how you would like to be in one year's time. What negative characteristics would you like to have left behind you? What spiritual qualities would you like to embody?*

2 *Use all the powers of your imagination to picture exactly who you would like to be and how you would like to be living and, most important, how this would feel.*

3 *Now let go of your desire and accept whatever life brings you in the faith that it will further your most spiritual aspirations.*

DREAM THE FUTURE INTO EXISTENCE

Dreams

EVERY NIGHT *we undertake a bizarre ritual. In a room that is set aside for the purpose, we undress, lie down on a special piece of furniture, rest our head on a pillow, and utterly change our state of awareness. The familiar world disappears and we emerge into a strange land where the laws of Nature can be arbitrarily broken, where we may or may not know those around us, and indeed may not even be ourselves. On average we dream for about ten to thirty minutes during ninety minutes of sleep. That's three to five dreaming periods a night. In a year that is about a thousand dreams. In an average lifetime that is over 70,000 dreams!*

EDGAR CAYCE

VALUABLE SPIRITUAL INFORMATION

For someone on the spiritual path this is valuable information that should not be wasted. The spiritual opportunities of everyday life are easily overlooked. Nowhere is this more true than with dreaming. Dreams give us an insight into those parts of ourselves that we are not yet ready to acknowledge consciously – both our dark side and our deeper spiritual nature.

LUCID DREAMING

In some dreams, dreamers are aware that they are dreaming. These are called "lucid dreams." Some people believe that in such dreams we are actually experiencing another dimension of reality sometimes called the Astral Plane. In some lucid dreams, dreamers leave their bodies and travel around the physical world – the so-called out-of-body experience. Many people claim that lucid dreams can be premonitions of coming events. A famous example is Edgar Cayce, known as the dreaming prophet, who made many predictions based on his dreams. In many traditions there are spiritual practices that cultivate the ability to dream lucidly. These practices help dreaming become an important aspect of one's spiritual life.

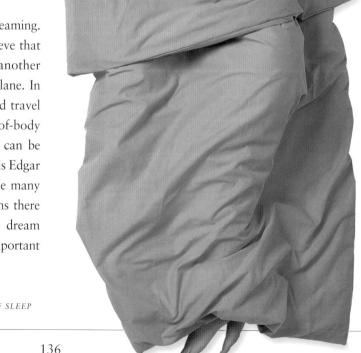

THE RITUAL OF SLEEP

The Power of Dreams

In shamanic cultures, dreams are taken very seriously. Families regularly share their dreams over breakfast. Dreams often reveal where game may be grazing, or dangers that may be about to afflict the tribe, or the hidden cause of some illness. The Native American visionary Black Elk tells us that a dream that was regarded as highly significant by the tribe would actually be acted out, with different people playing the roles of characters in the dream.

Dream Analysis

Modern psychoanalysis is a new approach to the old Pagan notion of healing through dream analysis. It was invented by Freud, who interpreted dreams as messages from the unconscious, mostly to do with sublimated sexuality. His protege, Carl Jung, expanded Freud's ideas considerably, giving them a spiritual context. Like the great mystics, Jung believed that we all share a collective unconscious. He plumbed the depths of this shared Mind and had many transformative spiritual experiences. Although for many years he was very wary about sharing these too openly for fear of being rejected by the scientific community, he ended his life more a mystical sage than a conventional scientist. Jung writes of his work with dreams:

THE TEMPLE OF APOLLO EPICURUS IN GREECE

"In each of us there is another whom we do not know. He speaks to us in dreams and tell us how differently he sees us from the way we see

NATIVE AMERICAN VISIONARY BLACK ELK

ourselves. When, therefore, we find ourselves in a difficult situation to which there is no solution, he can sometimes kindle a light that radically alters our attitude – the very attitude that led to the difficult situation."

Pagan Dreams

Ancient Egyptians and Greeks consulted the gods by sleeping in special rooms in a temple in order to receive divine guidance in their dreams. At his temple in Epidaurus, Asclepius, the god of healing, was believed to heal the sick through their dreams.

ASCLEPIUS, GOD OF MEDICINE AND HEALTH

THE NATIVE AMERICANS SLEPT UNDER "DREAMCATCHERS" WHICH ARE BELIEVED TO BRING CLEAR, POWERFUL DREAMS

A DREAM DIARY

The first problem in working with dreams is learning to recall them easily. A simple way of helping you do this is to keep a dream diary by your bed. When you go to sleep instill the intention in your mind that you wish to recall your dream. As soon as you wake up, immediately write down everything you remember of your dream. Over time you will find you remember more and more of your dreaming life with greater and greater vividness.

You may also like to experiment with holding a particular question in your mind before you go to sleep and ask your dreams to provide you with insights.

When you have had a dream that particularly strikes you, put aside some time to contemplate its meaning. A dream can be interpreted in many ways, so don't look for one definitive meaning. Allow the most relevant interpretation for the moment to arise.

Often it is enough just to spend time contemplating your dreams, without coming to any intellectual understanding of them, and let them work on you subliminally.

It can be helpful to share your dreams with a spiritual friend who can help you penetrate its meaning.

From time to time it is worth reviewing your dream diary and seeing if there is any pattern in your dreams. Are certain motifs constantly recurring for you? If so, what are they telling you?

Very vivid dream about being at a fairground on a big wheel. Then, I noticed that I was actually at the center of the wheel watching what looked like me going up and down and round and round. This image has really made a strong impression on me and I think I will use it as a focus for meditation later today.

NOTE DOWN YOUR INSIGHTS

66 While one is in the state of dream, the golden, self-luminous being, the Self within, the Immortal One, keeps alive the house of flesh, but at the same time walks out of this house. 99

BRIHADARANYAKA UPANISHAD
HINDU SCRIPTURE

❊❊❊❊

66 The self-luminous being assumes manifold forms in the world of dreams. He seems to be enjoying the pleasure of love, or to be laughing with friends, or to be looking at terrifying spectacles. Everyone is aware of the experiences. No one sees the Experiencer. 99

BRIHADARANYAKA UPANISHAD

❊❊❊❊

66 Our religion is the dreams of our old men, given to them in the solemn hours of the night by the Great Spirit; and the visions of our Medicine Men; and it is written in the hearts of the people. 99

CHIEF SEATTLE
NATIVE AMERICAN LEADER

❊❊❊❊

66 The unconscious is constantly producing teaching images. So, like the fabled lost continent, the wild dreamland rises out of our sleeping bodies.
It is the continent of our knowing.
It is the land of our Self. 99

CLARISSA PINKOLA ESTÉS
JUNGIAN ANALYST

Meditating on death

OVER 200,000 PEOPLE *died today and another 200,000 will die tomorrow. Sooner or later we will be one of them. This may seem to make our lives ultimately meaningless. But spirituality teaches that death is not to be feared and pushed to the back of our minds. It is a great teacher from whom we can learn the secrets of life. Many traditions encourage actively contemplating the inevitability of death. This is a challenging but rewarding spiritual practice. It forces us to go beyond any superficial ideas we may have of spirituality, which are inadequate before the enormity of death, and find something real.*

THE ANGEL GABRIEL

THE ULTIMATE CHALLENGE OF LIFE

Zen master Hakuin once boldly calligraphed the word "DEATH" and announced, "If anyone can see into the depths of this word he is a true hero." Death is the ultimate challenge of life. It is our final journey, which we must undertake alone. The Tibetan sage Drakpa Gyaltsen laments that, "Humans prepare for the future all their lives, yet meet the next life totally unprepared." Spirituality urges us not to ignore death but to focus on it. Death is not a meaningless tragedy, but the final initiation of life. The ancient Pagan sage Plato declared, "The best life is spent preparing for death."

ACKNOWLEDGING OUR MORTALITY

Dwelling on death is not macabre, it helps us realize the value of life. It stops us from deluding ourselves with a false sense of permanence. It forces us to question our identification with the mortal body and urges us to awaken an intuitive knowledge of the immortal soul. It teaches us not to become preoccupied with the transitory things of life that we must leave behind us, but rather to develop those spiritual qualities that become part of our inner nature. It reminds us to appreciate those we love and to seize the opportunity of life. It enables us to see clearly what is important and what is trivial. If we become conscious of the inevitability of death while we are healthy, then when illness and old age come it will not be a shocking surprise, but the expected fulfillment of life.

Buddhist Meditation on Death

66 With your heart contemplate the certainty that all your relations and all your wealth will be as nothing, like a deserted city. Everything is impermanent, so be detached.

With your heart contemplate the inevitability of death. When it comes, your home and possessions, your friends and famous colleagues, will not accompany you. Realize the absolute Truth. 99

KUNKYEN LONGCHEN RABJAM
TIBETAN BUDDHIST SAGE

A SYMBOL OF PURITY

Living with Death

In India and Tibet, monks and yogis often deliberately spend time in graveyards and the sites where the dead are cremated, surrounded by dead bodies. Sometimes they actually live in such places. Through this powerful spiritual practice they are forced to confront directly the transitory nature of their own bodies. A Buddhist scripture advises:

"If a monk sees a dead body that is one, two, or three days old, swollen, discolored, decomposing, thrown aside in the cemetery, he applies this perception to his own body, 'Truly, this body of mine, too, is of the same nature. It will become like that and will not escape it.'"

A PROCESSION TO A BUDDHIST CREMATION CEREMONY IN TIBET

Leaving Central Jail for Good

Many enlightened masters treat death very lightly, even flippantly. When admonished by his followers for dismissing the death of one of his devotees as if it were nothing, the Indian guru Neem Karoli Baba just smiled and replied, "Would you have me pretend that I am one of the puppets?" The day before his unexpected death he announced, "Tomorrow I'm leaving central jail for good."

The Last Announcement

Some masters have died actually sitting in meditation. Others predict their deaths or seem to choose exactly when they will leave the body. On the last day of his life Zen master Tanzan wrote 60 postcards that read:

"I am departing from this world.
This is my last announcement."

TANZAN, JULY 27. 1892

What's the Fuss?

It is traditional for Zen masters to write a final verse before their deaths. One master was almost passing away and had not performed this requirement, which his students pestered him to undertake. Eventually before letting out his last breath he reluctantly took a pen and scrawled:

"Life is thus, death is thus,
Verse or no verse, what's the fuss?"

CONTEMPLATING DEATH

A simple way of developing a spiritual awareness of death is to spend time regularly walking in a graveyard. Surrounded by monuments to those who have left this life, it is hard to avoid the sobering awareness of our own mortality.

As you walk, become aware that in life we are constantly surrounded by death. At first this can seem shocking – even terrifying. But acknowledging the transitory nature of everything focuses the mind on what really matters. Day-to-day worries and hassles suddenly become insignificant,

and the urgency of nurturing our spiritual awakening becomes obvious. Contemplating death shows us just how identified with the body we are. It reminds us that life is a precious opportunity not to be squandered.

A CEMETERY AT THE MOUNT OF OLIVES IN JERUSALEM

SHRINES IN RAJASTHAN, INDIA

66 Philosophy is nothing but a meditation on death. 99

SOCRATES
PAGAN SAGE

❀❀❀❀

66 The only remedy for the fear of death is to look it constantly in the face. 99

ATTAR
SUFI SAINT

❀❀❀❀

66 All the time I thought I was learning how to live, I was actually learning how to die. 99

LEONARDO DA VINCI
RENAISSANCE MYSTIC

❀❀❀❀

66 As a physician I am convinced that it is hygienic to discover in death a goal toward which one can strive, and that shrinking away from it is something unhealthy and abnormal that robs the second half of life of its meaning. 99

CARL JUNG
SCIENTIST AND SAGE

❀❀❀❀

66 There's no preparation for death except opening to the present. If you are here now, you'll be there then. 99

STEPHEN LEVINE
BUDDHIST TEACHER

❀❀❀❀

Ritual death

I N MANY SPIRITUAL *traditions, seekers undergo a form of ritual death to help them "die" to their ego-self and be reborn into an awareness of their true immortal nature. In the ancient Pagan Mystery religion, the initiates, known as "those about to die," were buried in a great trench, sometimes leaving only the head exposed. The Pagan initiate Lucius Apuleius describes himself as undergoing such a "voluntary death." These initiations often took place at midnight and would have been terrifying experiences. Through voluntarily undergoing ritual death, initiates overcome their fears and directly confront the profound mystery of their own existence.*

A SIOUX WARRIOR

DISMEMBERED BY SPIRITS

Rituals that simulate death are common in shamanic cultures. During the process of initiation in Siberia, the shaman lies unconscious for seven days and nights while he is said to be dismembered by spirits. In the Australian Aboriginal tradition the shaman, known as a "Karadji" or "Clever Man," undergoes a harrowing initiation of death and rebirth. It is said by some tribes that the Karadji goes to the mouth of a special cave where the spirits pierce him through the tongue, the neck, and from ear to ear with invisible spears. They then remove all his vital organs and replace them with magical quartz crystals.

THE NIGHT OF FEAR

The Native American Sioux have a practice called the "Night of Fear." In this ordeal the spiritual seeker goes out into the wilderness alone and digs a shallow grave in which to lie throughout the night. Without food or water, exposed to the elements and surrounded by the menacing darkness, the seeker's fears run amok – and with justification. Each sound could indeed be a

wild bear or a malevolent ghost. Here, lonely and filled with doubt, the seeker must face personal fears – especially the fear of death. The seeker may experience a mystical vision of Great Spirit, or be visited by a spirit animal that imparts spiritual teachings, or may receive a sacred song the seeker will be able to sing in future moments of desperation to reawaken the strength and courage discovered during the Night of Fear.

HARROWING HALLUCINATIONS

Those who undergo such initiations often report confrontations with terrifying demons. Tibetan Buddhists teach that such demons are manifestations of the initiate's own fears that are appearing so that they may be overcome. A Tibetan scripture known as "The Book of the Dead" teaches:

"Apart from one's own hallucinations, in reality there are no such things existing outside oneself as Lord of Death, or god, or demon, or the Bull-headed Spirit of Death. Act so as to recognize this."

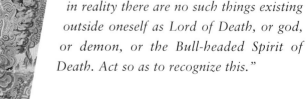

TIBETAN VISION OF HELL

"I Die Daily"

According to St. Paul, Christian baptism through total immersion in water is a type of ritual death in which entering the water signifies death, immersion beneath it means burial, and emergence from it is resurrection. Although such experiences mark a moment of symbolic transition in which the initiate dies to the old and is reborn as the new, St. Paul makes it clear that this process of dying and resurrecting must become a continuous experience. He writes, "I die daily." This is an ubiquitous spiritual teaching. The Zen masters similarly teach, "While alive, be a dead man." The Hindu saint Kabir writes, "It is they who are living yet dead that shall never die."

You Are Not a Person

The enlightened masters understand that the body is not our true identity. Having abandoned the "I am the body" idea, they have, in a sense, already died. For them the body is just another object in awareness. They have realized they are the witnessing Consciousness, which is undying because it was never born. Bodies come and go – Consciousness remains unchanging in eternity. The modern Hindu sage Sri Nisargadatta Maharaj teaches:

"You have squeezed yourself into the span of a lifetime and the volume of a body, and thus created the innumerable conflicts of life and death. Have your being outside this body of birth and death, and all your problems will be solved. They exist because you believe yourself born to die. Undeceive yourself and be free. You are not a person."

BAPTISM IN BARBADOS

MEDITATION ON A DECAYING CORPSE

Buddhists practice a meditation on death in which they imagine themselves to be a decaying corpse. This is not a practice for the fainthearted, but it is a powerful method of confronting our bodily mortality and so awakening an awareness of our immortal spirit.

You may like to perform the following meditation with a friend who will read out the stages of the visualization to you. Leave plenty of time between each stage.

✺ *Lie down with your hands by your side and completely relax in a dark room or with only the light of a candle.*

✺ *Imagine that you are a corpse that has recently died.*

✺ *Imagine that the corpse is now cold and rigid.*

✺ *Imagine that the corpse is turning blue.*

✺ *Imagine cracks appearing in the skin.*

✺ *Imagine parts of the body are beginning to decompose.*

✺ *Imagine the whole body is decomposing.*

✺ *Imagine the corpse is now a skeleton with odd pieces of decaying flesh still adhering to it.*

✺ *Imagine all that now exists is a pile of bones.*

✺ *Imagine that the bones are reduced to a handful of dust.*

✺ *Imagine the dust is blown way by the wind leaving nothing at all.*

✺ *Who are "you" now?*

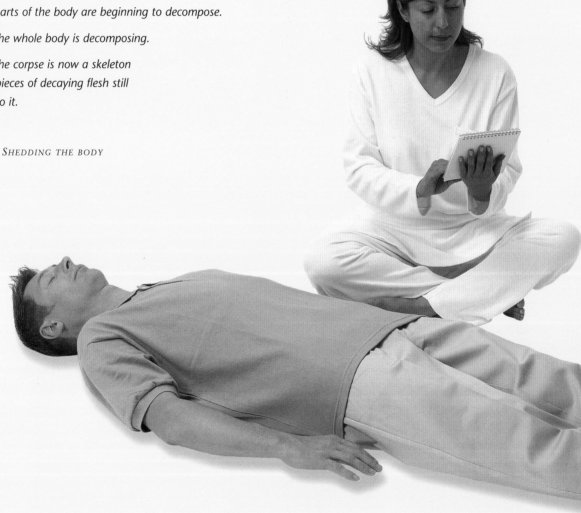

SHEDDING THE BODY

Song of Myself

❝ Has anyone supposed it lucky to be born?
I hasten to inform him or her it is just as lucky to die,
and I know it.
I pass death with the dying, and birth with the
new-washed babe ... and am not contained
between my hat and boots. ❞

WALT WHITMAN

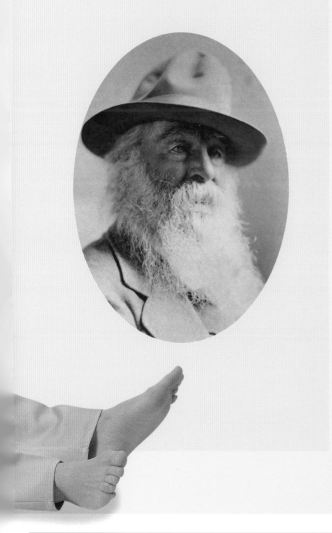

❝ What is it to die but to stand naked in the wind
and to melt into the sun? What is it to cease breathing
but to free the breath from its restless tides, that it may
rise and seek God unencumbered? ❞

KAHLIL GIBRAN
POET AND MYSTIC

❄❄❄❄

❝ That's why my Father loves me,
because I lay down my life to get it back again. ❞

JESUS
GOSPEL OF JOHN

❄❄❄❄

❝ That 'corpse' you dread so much
is living with you right here and now! ❞

MILAREPA
TIBETAN BUDDHIST SAGE

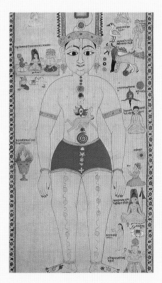

*INDIAN REPRESENTATION
OF ENERGIES SURROUNDING
THE PHYSICAL BODY*

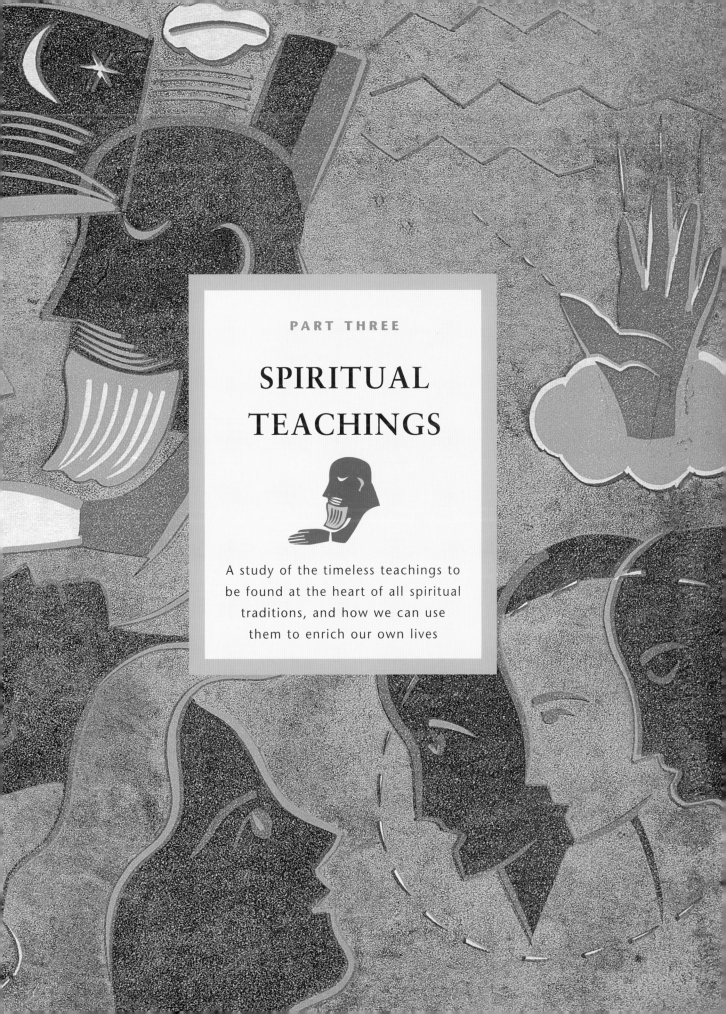

PART THREE

SPIRITUAL
TEACHINGS

A study of the timeless teachings to
be found at the heart of all spiritual
traditions, and how we can use
them to enrich our own lives

SPIRITUAL TEACHINGS

THIS SECTION OF THE BOOK *explores the perennial teachings found at the heart of all spiritual traditions and how we can apply them in our own lives.* To understand these teachings it is necessary to have a clear grasp of the relationship between religion, spirituality, and mysticism. These three related but distinct levels of understanding are often progressively experienced by seekers during their journey of awakening. An interest in religion often leads a seeker to the spiritual path. An understanding of mysticism is what enables them to stop traveling and finally arrive.

THE RUSSIAN PHILOSOPHER AND
SPIRITUAL MASTER G. I. GURDJIEFF

" The Way is fundamentally the same for everyone.

Its essence is to awaken

without this being an achievement.

Even saying the word 'awaken'

creates waves on still waters.

This is even more true with teachings and sayings.

If you grasp the leftovers

you cannot hold to reality

and will end up cut off from the Source. "

BASSUI
ZEN MASTER

RELIGION

Religion is concerned with rituals, observances, creeds, and codes of social morality. It marks the transitions of life, such as birth, marriage, and death, with appropriate rites that bind together a community. Religion is the outer form of spirituality. However, it is perfectly possible to be religious but not spiritual. Many people piously participate in religious customs without ever undertaking a personal journey of spiritual transformation. Fundamentalism of all persuasions, with its insistence on blind faith in dogmas, is religion without true spirituality. This is why it so often divides people instead of uniting them.

SPIRITUALITY

Spirituality is the inner content of all religions, but it does not necessarily have to have a religious context. Spirituality is about setting out on a personal search for answers to the most profound questions of life. Spirituality is a journey of awakening to who we really are; a journey of opening the heart to the love that permeates the universe; a journey from confusion to meaning; a journey from fear to faith; a journey from ennui to a life filled with magic and wonder; a journey from feeling alone in a hostile world to being at one with everyone and everything.

STONEHENGE ON SALISBURY PLAIN, ENGLAND, THE SITE OF RITUALS IN PREHISTORIC TIMES

MYSTICISM

Mysticism is the deepest level of spirituality. It teaches that reality is an indivisible Whole appearing as many parts. Although we think of ourselves as separate individuals, this is an illusion. There is only the constantly metamorphosing Totality. We are not the transitory mortal beings we take ourselves to be. Our immortal and eternal Self is one with the Oneness.

SEEMING, BECOMING, BEING

To go beyond religion we must realize that it is not enough to seem to be good, rather we must set out on the spiritual journey to actually become good. To reach our destination we must realize that it is not enough to be continually becoming a better person. Rather we must relinquish the idea of ourselves as a person altogether. We must dissolve the separate self into the impersonal Oneness and be the Goodness that is God.

THE PARADOX OF THE SPIRITUAL PATH

Spirituality takes religion to a deeper level. It teaches us that it is not enough simply to accept religious dogmas. We must undergo a process of personal transformation so that we directly experience the truth of these teachings for ourselves. Mysticism takes spirituality to a deeper level. It leads the seeker to the ultimate goal of spirituality, sometimes called "liberation" or "enlightenment" or "communion with God." The enigmatic riddle at the very epicenter of spirituality is that, to arrive at this experience of Oneness, we must realize that the idea of being a "someone" walking the spiritual path is itself just a fantasy produced by the illusion of separateness.

ZEN MASTER THICH NHAT HANH LEADS A WALKING MEDITATION IN NATURE

Religion is concerned with social cohesion.
Spirituality is concerned with personal transformation.
Mysticism is concerned with impersonal enlightenment.

❋❋❋❋❋❋❋

Religion is concerned with knowing about God.
Spirituality is concerned with personally experiencing God.
Mysticism is concerned with being one with God.

❋❋❋❋❋❋❋

Spirituality is the essence of religion.
Mysticism is the essence of spirituality.

A PAINTING AT AMRITSAR, INDIA, SHOWING A SIKH HOLY MAN RECEIVING PILGRIMS

LIVING TEACHINGS
AND DEAD DOGMAS

Spiritual traditions have characteristically developed from the insights of great saints and sages who have tried to pass on something of their mystical experience of enlightenment. After the deaths of these remarkable individuals, most traditions have constantly had to wrestle with the tendency for living teachings, designed to bring about spiritual transformation, to stultify into dead dogmas, designed to provide religious security to the unquestioning. For anyone interested in spirituality, rather than religion, the task is to rediscover the true spirit and meaning of the teachings, and to avoid getting bogged down in religious creeds. Otherwise, rather than setting us free, the tradition traps us in a new type of prison.

PERENNIAL TEACHINGS

Although the enlightened masters each have their unique perspective on the human predicament, their essential message is extremely similar. The sorry history of bloody conflict between competing religions has left many people with the impression that humanity's various spiritual traditions are irreconcilably in conflict with each other, but this is not so. Underneath the superficial differences created by conflicting conceptual vocabularies we find the same core teachings. This shared understanding is not comprised of religious dogmas to be believed or disputed, but insights to be critically contemplated and techniques that aid our awakening to be tested out in our own lives. To understand human spirituality is to appreciate the rich variety of expression given to a universal and perennial wisdom.

Teachings on Two Levels

Spirituality is a process of personal transformation that prepares us for the spontaneous experience of impersonal enlightenment in which the separate self is seen to be an illusion. The spiritual teachings and practices we explore in this section of the book address both these levels of understanding. They guide us through the challenges we face on our personal spiritual path, but at the same time they chip away at our concept of ourselves as "a someone going somewhere."

PLATO AND ARISTOTLE

66 Someone who seeks for anything in religion other than God and the salvation of his soul will find nothing there but sorrow and trouble. 99

THOMAS À KEMPIS
CHRISTIAN SAGE

❄❄❄❄

66 The mystics speak in a hundred different ways, but if God is one and the Way is one, how could their meaning be other than one? What appears in different disguises is one essence. A variety of expression, but the same meaning. 99

JALAL AL-DIN RUMI
SUFI SAGE

❄❄❄❄

66 If you hold to a particular perspective, you don't have the correct perspective. 99

GÜNPA NYINGPO
BUDDHIST SAGE

❄❄❄❄

66 God does not reserve the high vocation of mystical contemplation for certain souls only. On the contrary He wants all to embrace it, but finds few who will permit Him to work such exalted things for them. 99

ST. JOHN OF THE CROSS
CHRISTIAN MYSTIC

The spiritual path

EACH ONE OF US *was born and one day will die. Between these two extraordinary events is the mysterious process we call "life." It is very easy to get so caught up in the daily chores necessary to maintain our existence that we go about our business as if life were nothing special at all. Spirituality, however, reminds us that life is something special. It is a wonderful experience to be enjoyed. It is a great enigma to be solved. It is a precious opportunity to be seized. And it is passing away right now.*

THE MIRACLE
OF LIFE

THE JOURNEY OF AWAKENING

Spirituality teaches that the purpose of life is to undertake the journey of spiritual awakening. Just as we wake up each morning from our physical sleep, we need to wake up further from our spiritual sleep. In some spiritual traditions, life is compared to a school in which we are willing or unwilling students. The syllabus is comprised of our everyday trials and tribulations. Death is our final opportunity to graduate. Sometimes life is likened to a hospital in which we are patients, recovering from the sickness of spiritual ignorance, or even a prison in which we languish as a result of misdeeds in past lives, from which we can escape only by attaining spiritual liberation.

A DIVINE MISSION

Many traditions picture us as having been sent to earth on a divine mission by God. The Islamic Sufi sage Jalal al-Din Rumi compares our predicament to being emissaries sent to a foreign land by a king who has entrusted us to perform a specific task. Unfortunately, however, we have forgotten our mission and become embroiled with a thousand and one distractions. This divinely ordained mission that we must not forget is to spiritually awaken.

Daily Opportunities for Initiation

Walking the spiritual path is not just about setting aside time for regular spiritual practice. It is about transforming all of life into a spiritual practice. The spiritual path is not a part of life. It is understanding that all the challenges of daily existence are our opportunities to be initiated into deeper levels of spiritual understanding.

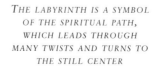

THE LABYRINTH IS A SYMBOL
OF THE SPIRITUAL PATH,
WHICH LEADS THROUGH
MANY TWISTS AND TURNS TO
THE STILL CENTER

INADEQUATE ALLEGORIES

Such myths give a context to the joys and sufferings of our existence, but they are ultimately inadequate allegories. Even the notions of life being a "spiritual path" or a "journey of awakening" are only crude metaphors. Actually the "meaning of life" can only be intuitively grasped in moments of deep mystical insight. From the enlightened perspective life neither has a purpose nor is it purposeless. It just is what it is.

A Pilgrimage We Will Never Complete

The spiritual adventure is an inner drama played out in the theater of the world. It is our personal struggle to discover the impersonal Oneness. It is a pilgrimage that we will never complete, for it is ultimately our sense of being a separate self that stands between us and our goal. If we do not realize this from the outset, the journey of awakening can itself become a more subtle form of spiritual sleep. We may succeed in becoming more "holy," but we will never experience the Wholeness. Spirituality is not about becoming a more spiritual person, it is ultimately about discovering we are not a person at all. Without this understanding, spirituality may make our lives more bearable by helping us rearrange the furniture in our prison cell, but it will not set us free.

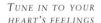

TUNE IN TO YOUR HEART'S FEELINGS

LIVING THE LIFE YOU WANT TO LIVE

This contemplation exercise can help you clarify whether you are living the life you want to be living or whether you need to make some changes.

1 *Focus your mind in contemplation and ask yourself "Am I living the life I really want to live?" "Am I being the sort of person I really want to be?" Don't just accept a superficial response. Really search your heart and uncover your true feelings.*

2 *Imagine yourself on your death bed looking back over your life. What would make you feel that your life had been worthwhile? What would make you feel that your life had been wasted?*

3 *The understanding you gain may make you want to change aspects of the way you are living your life. If you regularly tune into your heart's deepest desire, it will give you the motivation and energy you need to transform yourself and your life.*

GATEWAY TO THE SOUL

Walking the spiritual path is a process of coming to Consciousness, of becoming ever more aware until we begin to become aware of Awareness itself. Performing this exercise with a spiritual friend is a powerful way of becoming conscious of our own Consciousness by recognizing the same mysterious presence within someone else.

1 *Sit comfortably and gaze into one another's eyes. The eyes are the gateway to the soul. Let your awareness pass through this gateway.*

2 *Focus on the deep dark circle of the pupil at the center of the eye and become aware of an intangible presence that is gazing back at you from the nothingness. Sense that here is another Consciousness – just like you.*

As you develop the ability to see beyond the eyes you can play with this awareness anywhere and anytime. When you are in the supermarket buying your groceries, for example, don't just see the cashier as a stranger taking your money. Also be aware of the mystery of Consciousness behind his or her eyes. The other person does not need to be aware that you are doing this, but you will find that this silent acknowledgment makes something special out of even the most mundane of human interactions.

It is not only human beings who are conscious, so you can also experiment with searching out the Consciousness behind the eyes of animals. You can also simply stare at your own eyes in a mirror and reach beyond your own appearance to the ineffable Consciousness it conceals.

*CONNECTING WITH
ANOTHER CONSCIOUSNESS*

❝ Human beings come into this world for a particular purpose, and if they forget it they will have done nothing at all. ❞

JALAL AL-DIN RUMI
SUFI SAGE

❧❧❧❧

Zen master Zuigan would greet himself
each morning and request of himself
"Today please try to wake up,"
to which he would answer, "Yes, indeed I will."

❝ The human being is an animal who has received the vocation to become God. ❞

BASIL OF CAESAREA
CHRISTIAN SAGE

❧❧❧❧

❝ Is some sickness coming tonight?
Is death waiting for us tomorrow?
There is no greater folly
than to be alive but unconscious –
not following the Buddha's Way. ❞

THE VENERABLE CHING
BUDDHIST SAGE

PILGRIMS AT PRAYER

The Life Power

DIFFERENT SPIRITUAL TRADITIONS *express themselves in different conceptual vocabularies, but essentially all of them are pointing to the one Truth. There is a Life Force that permeates all of creation. There is a Supreme Power that orchestrates the symphony of life. There is an ultimate Oneness that subsumes all things within it. There is an unconditional Love that embraces everyone equally without discrimination. There is a mysterious Presence that in moments of quiet or exaltation we can sense around us and within us.*

BUDDHA

A PERSONAL GOD

Many traditions conceive of the Life Power as a personal God who is the creator of all things. Some traditions, such as Christianity, picture God as a divine Father who guides us with a firm but loving hand. Other traditions, such as the indigenous shamanic religions, picture God as a divine Mother who nurtures and provides for us from her maternal bounty. For others still, such as the Islamic Sufi tradition, God is a spiritual lover or spouse. For the Hindu saint Kabir, God is simply the "Friend." All of these images project a human face onto the Higher Power and so enable us to experience an intimate emotional relationship with the ineffable Oneness.

AN IMPERSONAL POWER

Such anthropomorphic pictures of a personal God are attractive, but ultimately limit the limitless grandeur of the Power of Life. As the ancient Egyptian sage Hermes Trismegistus puts it, "To define God is impossible. For God is too great to be even called by the name 'God.'" Some spiritual traditions respond to this dilemma by using impersonal language. Lao Tzu talks of the Tao or the "Way." The Zen master Yung-chia Ta-shih writes of "one perfect Nature pervading and circulating within all natures, one all-inclusive Reality containing and embracing all realities."

MICHELANGELO'S THE CREATION OF ADAM

THE GREAT MYSTERY

Even abstract conceptions, however, are only attempts to describe the indescribable. The infinite Life Power cannot be constrained by names and ideas. The Hindu sage Sankara calls it "the One before whom words recoil." Jewish mystics of the Middle Ages called God by the title "Mi," which means "The Who?" Hindu mystics, likewise, use the title "Ka," which also means "Who?" The Life Power is necessarily inscrutable and completely beyond our comprehension. How can a part possibly comprehend the Whole? Native Americans speak of "The Great Mystery," and it is perhaps best to leave it at that. As the Taoist sage Lao Tzu puts it:

"Tao is mystery. This is the gateway to understanding."

"An unchanging Oneness.

An ever-changing Presence.

An indefinable Original Totality.

It is impossible to really give it a name,

but I call it 'Tao.'"

LAO TZU
TAOIST SAGE

❧❧❧❧

"He is hidden yet obvious everywhere.

He is bodiless yet embodied in everything.

There is nothing which he is not.

He has no name because all names are his name.

He is the unity in all things,

so we must know him by all names

and call everything 'God.'"

HERMES TRISMEGISTUS
ANCIENT EGYPTIAN SAGE

❧❧❧❧

"For those who look with their physical eyes,

God is nowhere to be seen.

For those who contemplate Him in spirit,

He is everywhere.

He is in all, yet beyond all."

SYMEON
CHRISTIAN SAINT

❧❧❧❧

"Meditate and realize that this world

is full of the presence of God."

SHVETASHVATARA UPANISHAD
HINDU SCRIPTURE

SENSING THE PRESENCE

There is no need to sit in meditation to become aware of the Life Force. It is always with you. It is around you right now. As you go about your daily business be conscious of the Power of Life as a mysterious presence permeating the universe. Be attentive to LIFE pulsing everywhere, every moment, in everyone and everything.

A CONVERSATION WITH YOUR CREATOR

Experiment with perceiving your life as an intimate dialogue between yourself and your Creator. Instead of viewing all that happens to you as "ordinary" or "coincidental," treat every event as a message from the Great Mystery. It doesn't matter whether you see this as a personal God or the impersonal Tao, just ask yourself "What is it saying to me?"

BE CONSCIOUS OF THE MYSTERY WHEN LIVING YOUR EVERYDAY LIFE

Ramakrishna

The Hindu saint Ramakrishna (1836–86) spent most of his life in mystical rapture and was known as "the madman of God." He saw God in everyone and everything, and viewed all religions as different paths to one divine destination.

"I have practiced all religions – Hinduism, Islam, Christianity – and I have also followed the paths of various sects of Hinduism. I have found that it is the same God toward whom all are turned, all along different roads. Everywhere I see men who dispute in the name of religion. But they do not stop to think that he who is called Krishna is also called Shiva, and that he is also called Primal Force or Jesus or Allah. The substance is One under different names, and each man is looking for the same substance."

God Alone Is

Ramakrishna was a devotee and priest in the cult of the goddess Kali, whom he called the Divine Mother. Later he studied Vedantic Hindu philosophy and came to combine the paths of Bhakti and Gnana – devotion and knowledge. For Ramakrishna, God was not somewhere up in heaven. Nor was he found only by looking within. Actually, God is everything that is. There is only God.

"A poor devotee points to the sky and says ,'God is up there.' An average devotee says ,'God dwells in the heart as the Inner Master.' The best devotee says ,'God alone is ,and everything I perceive is a form of God.'"

THE HINDU GOD KRISHNA
WITH A DEVOTEE

KALI

Hinduism for Westerners

Ramakrishna became internationally famous through his disciple Vivekananda (1863–1902). He took Ramakrishna's teachings to the world and was one of the first teachers to attract large numbers of disillusioned Westerners to Hindu spirituality. Vivekananda also saw God in all. He taught:

"Every man and women is the palpable, blissful, living God. Who says God is unknown? Who says he is to be searched for? We have found God eternally. We have been living in Him eternally."

Self-knowledge

To those who *asked him for spiritual teachings, the Hindu sage Ramana Maharshi would often simply respond, "Who is asking?" The spiritual masters urge us to set out on a journey of self-discovery, which begins with the fundamental question "Who am I?" Materialism teaches that we are just a skin-bag full of blood and guts that happens to be conscious, but which is destined to die and be recycled into other forms of organic life. Spirituality, on the other hand, teaches that our essential nature is not physical at all. We are immortal consciousness that has temporally incarnated in a physical form.*

A TEMPORARY STATE

A CONSCIOUS BODY OR EMBODIED CONSCIOUSNESS?

Are we a conscious body or embodied consciousness? In a sense, the answer is both. The body and personality that make up our separate identity are indeed transitory phenomena that will live and die. But the essential Consciousness that animates us – our sense of "I am" – is not a thing at all. This is our true identity, sometimes called the spirit or higher Self. However, most of the time Consciousness mistakenly identifies itself with the body and personality it inhabits. This false identity is often called the lower self or ego. Spirituality is about transcending our false identity and being what we truly are – eternal pure Consciousness.

BEING A GENIUS

The Pagan sages of antiquity called our true identity the "Genius." They called the ego-self that we mistakenly take ourselves to be the "idolon," which means "shadow." The ego-self is a shadow cast by the light of the Genius. Sometimes the ancients referred to it as the "persona," a word derived from the name for a ritual mask. The "persona," or as we say today "personality," is a mask worn by the true Self. It is how we appear to be. The Genius is what we are.

THE ATMAN AND THE JIVA

The Hindu masters call the witnessing Consciousness, which is our true identity, the "Atman" and the ego-self the "jiva." The yogi Vasishtha writes:

"Regard your body and sense as instruments for experiencing, not as your true Self. It is when pure Consciousness, the 'Atman,' gives rise to concepts and notions within itself that it assumes an individuality, the 'jiva.' Such individuals wander in the illusionary world of appearances. Even so, it is possible to perceive through the individual's experiences the pure experiencing, which is the infinite Consciousness. But this Self-knowledge is not gained by study of the scriptures or with the help of a guru. It can only be gained by the Self for itself."

THE PERSONALITY IS A MASK WORN BY PURE CONSCIOUSNESS

I AM THE UNTHINKABLE

The spiritual masters teach that we are not who we think we are. What we think we are is just a thought. A conceptual picture. An idea in Consciousness. What we are is the Consciousness that is conscious of the thought. However, the realization "I am not who I think I am" is infinitely regressive. Even the conclusion "I am the Consciousness that is conscious of thoughts" is only an idea in Consciousness. Anything that we think we are is only an idea. What we are in reality cannot be known with thoughts. We can only be what we really are.

I AM GOD

Our true identity cannot be conceived of by the mind. It is as mysterious and inscrutable as the Power of Life that animates everything. Indeed, the great mystics teach that our true ineffable Self is the Power of Life. We are actually the one Consciousness of the Universe, witnessing the unfolding of life through a particular body. Such teachings are ubiquitous in Eastern traditions such as Hinduism, Buddhism, and Taoism. But they are also found in Christianity and Islam. The Islamic Sufi saint Mahmud Shabistari explains, "There is only one light of Consciousness, and 'you' and 'me' are holes in the lamp shade." The great Christian mystic Meister Eckhart writes, "Our truest 'I' is God."

KNOWING THE KNOWER

In the Hindu tradition an enlightened master is called a "Gnani." The Buddhists use the title "Buddha." The early Christian tradition used the term "Gnostic." All of these words mean "Knower." What is it the enlightened masters know? Although these remarkable human beings may indeed be extremely well informed about spiritual matters, it is not this that makes them a "Knower." To become a "Knower" is to know one's true Self. To know that which does the knowing. To be the Knower – the experiencing Consciousness.

SPIRITUALITY TEACHES THAT WHO WE NORMALLY TAKE OURSELVES TO BE IS ONLY AN IMAGE OF OUR TRUE IDENTITY

THE AWARENESS OF "I AM"

Many spiritual masters teach that the most direct path to awakening lies in simply becoming aware of our own beingness – our sense of "I am." Although this sounds easy enough, it is actually not so straightforward. This pure sense of being is habitually confused with all sorts of extraneous ideas about who we are and what we are. Only by purifying our sense of "I am" from all of these accretions can we begin to glimpse our naked essence.

1 *Let go of all your ideas about what you are and concentrate on the certain knowledge that you are. Focus your attention on your sense of "I am"; your very essence; the brute fact of your existence.*

2 *As you do this, it will become obvious that there are no words to describe this ineffable sense of being. It has no qualities. It is not your body. All bodily sensations are passing phenomena witnessed by the "I." It is not your mind or feelings. These too are phenomena that the "I" experiences.*

3 *The "I" is the experiencer of all that you experience, but it itself cannot be experienced. As you struggle to know the "I," you will find it cannot be known. It is the knower. It is what you are. You cannot know yourself, you can only be yourself.*

66 Through the power of habit I have come to view an insignificant sperm and egg as myself. 99

SHANTIDEVA
BUDDHIST SAGE

❦❦❦❦

66 Names and ideas create the ego.

This blocks your perception of the Great Oneness,

therefore it is wise to ignore them. 99

HUA HU CHING
TAOIST SAGE

❦❦❦❦

66 I am nothing,

for all that I am

is no more than an image of Being,

and only God is my I AM. 99

JACOB BOEHME
CHRISTIAN MYSTIC

❦❦❦❦

66 Those who realize the Self are always satisfied. Having found the source of joy and fulfillment they no longer seek happiness from the external world. They have nothing to gain or lose by any action; neither people nor things can affect their security. 99

BHAGAVAD GITA
HINDU SCRIPTURE

66 I am the adjective of some transcendental Self. 99

T S ELIOT
MYSTIC AND POET

Selflessness

*S*PIRITUALITY TEACHES THAT, *paradoxically, only through selflessness will we find personal fulfillment. Being obsessed with our ego-self cannot lead to the happiness we all crave, because it is this obsession that is the cause of our unhappiness. To serve the separate self is ultimately self-defeating, because this is not who we are. Selfishness cuts us off from our true identity and binds us tightly to the transitory world of loss and suffering.*

NO ONE
THERE

SELFISHNESS IS STUPID

When we are selfish it is not just bad for those around us. It is also bad for us. Selfishness is a stupid way to live our lives, because it doesn't bring us the rewards we hope for. Ultimately it brings us only isolation and suffering.

BENEFITING OTHERS BENEFITS OURSELVES

The mysterious secret taught by the spiritual masters is that by benefiting others we benefit ourselves and by harming others we harm ourselves. Graciously giving our time and attention to those less able to cope with life, leaves us feeling stronger. Not being bothered when others need us leaves us without friends. Sharing our possessions and money with those less well-off leaves us feeling richer. Hoarding what we own leaves us without anyone to turn to if times get hard for us. Making a special effort to be sensitive to people around us leaves us feeling more alive. Being insensitive leaves us feeling numb. The simple truth is that being selfless makes us feel better about ourselves.

THE SELFLESS SELF?

But is it possible to be really selfless? Being aware of the needs of others may make us better people, but we are still caught in a curious predicament. For anything we think we do, whether we believe it to be selfish or selfless, inevitably endorses our notion of being a separate individual. This is why the enlightened masters teach us that ultimately it is not enough to polish up the ego in the hope of becoming a selfless self.

66 We say that 'Good' and 'Harmony,' and 'Evil' and 'Disharmony' are synonymous. Further we maintain that illness, pain, and suffering are results of want of Harmony, and that the one terrible and only cause to the disturbance of Harmony is selfishness in some form or another. 99

HELENA BLAVATSKY

MADAME HELENA BLAVATSKY, FOUNDER OF *THE THEOSOPHICAL SOCIETY*

EVERYONE IS SELFISH AND NO ONE IS SELFISH

To be really selfless is to understand that the separate self is an illusion. To act selflessly, therefore, is to know that there is no "you" that acts, but only God acting in all things. This understanding leaves us with another intriguing spiritual paradox. As long as we believe ourselves to be a separate self it is actually impossible not to act selfishly, yet from the mystical perspective there are no separate selves and therefore no one to act selfishly or otherwise.

66 Love is selflessness, self is lovelessness. 99

SAI BABA
HINDU GURU

❦❦❦❦

66 The one work we should rightly undertake is eradication of the self. Could you completely forget yourself, even for just an instant, you would be given everything. 99

MEISTER ECKHART
CHRISTIAN SAGE

ST. GREGORY

AWARENESS OF OTHERS

Often the simplest of all spiritual practices are the most profound. The most obvious way of escaping the prison of the ego is simply to reach out to others.

Decide today to be particularly conscious of the needs and desires of those around you and to ask yourself what you can contribute to others' happiness and well-being.

This does not have to entail grand gestures. Everyday we are surrounded by people in need of just a kind word, a helping hand, or a friendly smile.

Be aware of how reaching beyond yourself affects your relationship with others and how it changes your experience of yourself.

PRACTICE SMALL ACTS OF COMPASSION

Love

HE ESSENTIAL TEACHING of spirituality is that to find fulfillment we must transcend our separate self. The easiest way of doing this is by simply opening the heart to love. Many people are walking this path in their lives without ever bothering to trouble themselves with spiritual philosophy or burdening their lives with the need for spiritual practices – and they are none the poorer for this. Love is the natural way for human beings to awaken spiritually. Love enough and all the great teachings of spirituality will reveal themselves spontaneously.

WE ALL NEED LOVE

GOD IS LOVE

To truly love is to enter a holy communion in which we transcend our individual existence and partake in a greater identity. Like a spiritual analogue of that mysterious force of material attraction we call gravity, love seeks unity. In their different ways, all spiritual traditions teach that "God is love." This is because Oneness and love are different ways of describing the same Great Mystery. Love is how Oneness feels. It is how we experience the paradox of being an individual part of an indivisible Whole.

LOVE IS THE MOTIVATION

Love is what gives meaning to human life. Without love, life is barren and futile. At root everything is motivated by love. Our selfishness is fueled by our love of our separate self. Our materialism is driven by our love of luxury and pleasure. Our spiritual quest is fired by our love for God or Truth or Life itself. Our loving may be small and self-orientated or may expand to envelop the whole universe.

AN ABUNDANCE OF LOVE

We all need love. It is a fundamental part of human nature to crave to escape the loneliness of our separate existence and connect with others and all of life. Yet most people feel the world to be a love-impoverished place. The great mystics teach that this is only because we focus on having our selfish needs met rather than on loving itself. Love, by its very nature, is found when we escape the ego-self. When we do, we find ourselves held in an embrace so big it is without limits. We discover a cosmos permeated by compassion. A love that has no reason and applies no conditions. A love that loves for its own sake.

LOVE IS NATURAL

The Dalai Lama

His Holiness the Dalai Lama (see below) is the spiritual leader of Tibetan Buddhism. Up until the Chinese occupation in 1959 he was also the ruler of Tibet. He is believed to be a Boddhisattva – a master who has reincarnated over and over again to bring all beings to enlightenment. He is also an incarnation of Avalokiteshvara, the Buddha of Compassion. The Dalai Lama teaches us to have compassion for all sentient beings. He even preaches compassion toward the Chinese who are destroying his country and oppressing his people. Only love can transform horror

TIBETAN MANDALA

and hate into harmony and reconciliation. The Dalai Lama teaches, "My religion is kindness." To be kind is to acknowledge that we are all one family, that we are "kindred," that we are all animated by the one Life Force. The Dalai Lama teaches us to treat all other beings with kindness, as if they were already our close friends. This is a more palatable adaptation of the traditional Tibetan teaching that we should love all other beings as if they were our mother, because we have undergone so many incarnations that in some previous existence they probably were our mother!

LOVING KINDNESS MEDITATION

Buddhists cultivate compassion through a meditation practice known as the "metabhavana" or "loving kindness meditation." This involves sitting silently with eyes closed for about 20 minutes while successively bringing to mind someone you find it easy to love, then someone toward whom you feel indifferent, then someone you find difficult to love, and finally yourself. Ironically, people often find this last stage the most difficult of all, but unless we can love ourselves, it is impossible to really love others – because in Truth we are all One.

1 *First focus your thoughts on someone whom you find it very easy to love – a friend, parent, child, lover, anyone at all. Concentrate on the feelings that you experience when you become aware of how much you love that person. Remember times you have shared when you have felt particularly full of love. Bathe in the love that you feel.*

2 *After about five minutes bring to mind someone to whom you are indifferent – a stranger you pass in the street each day, a colleague at work, the postman, anyone toward whom you do not particularly feel anything at all. Consider that he or she is a sentient being, just like you, who experiences all the joys and sufferings of life. Remember that even your best friend was once a stranger like this person is now. Open your heart and extend your feelings of loving kindness to embrace this person also.*

3 *After about five minutes bring to mind someone whom you have exiled from your*

heart – someone with whom you have quarreled, someone who you feel has wronged you, anyone whom you find it difficult to love. Remember how easy it is for all of us to act badly and consider that everyone has his or her side of the story. Sense this person's true Self, which, although it may be trapped within a dysfunctional personality, is all goodness and is crying out to be recognized. Extend your feelings of loving kindness further and take this person also into your heart. Do not criticize yourself if you find this difficult, but gently work to bring down the barriers that keep your heart closed.

4 *After about five minutes turn your attention to yourself and surround yourself with loving kindness. Reach out with your heart to yourself as if you were comforting your closest friend or most intimate lover. Wish yourself well. Honor what is good in you and forgive yourself for all your failings.*

"There are no obstacles.
The great gate of compassion is wide open."

YUNG-CHIA TA-SHIH
ZEN MASTER

❀❀❀❀

"God is love
and those that live in love live in God
and God lives in them."

ST. JOHN
THE NEW TESTAMENT

❀❀❀❀

"Only if one knows the truth of love, which is the
real nature of Self, will the strong entangled knot of life
be untied. Only if one attains the height of love will
liberation be attained. Such is the heart of all religions.
The experience of Self is only love – which is seeing
only love, hearing only love, feeling only love, tasting
only love, and smelling only love, which is bliss."

RAMANA MAHARSHI
HINDU SAGE

❀❀❀❀

"Love is the answer,
and you know that for sure."

MIND GAMES
JOHN LENNON

Personal growth

SPIRITUALITY IS PROFOUNDLY *paradoxical. To walk the spiritual path we must become a better person, yet to reach the destination of enlightenment we must "unbecome" a person altogether. The spirituality path is a process of weeding out those quirks of character that act as obstacles to our awakening and in their place cultivating helpful, wholesome personal qualities. This loosens our attachments to the ego-self and so allows the possibility of enlightenment spontaneously occurring.*

CONFRONTING THE SHADOW

To walk the spiritual path requires intense critical introspection. We must be willing to acknowledge and confront our "shadow" side if we are going to grow spiritually. Ironically, as we work on ourselves, the light of our growing awareness shows up previously hidden dark recesses where lurk unwholesome aspects of our personality that we would prefer to ignore. These negative personality quirks are more than obstacles we must navigate. They are precious opportunities to awaken. They are the bonds that tie us to the ego, which we must throw off if we are to become free. The more spiritually mature we become, the more we cease to look away from our failings and instead begin actively to seek them out. Those who want to be free are eager to become aware of exactly what is binding them.

SPIRITUALITY, BY CATHERINE McINTYRE

SPIRITUAL IMMATURITY

We work on the self so that ultimately we are able to transcend it altogether. Through the process of personal growth, the ego matures spiritually. Eventually it becomes like a ripe fruit that naturally falls from the tree. Like a fruit, before we are ripe we are bitter. It is no good resenting this in others or in ourselves. Only ripe fruit are really sweet. It is just the natural way of things. Personal failings are an unavoidable byproduct of spiritual immaturity. The spiritually ripe self is the fulfillment of the gradual process of maturation. But once it has ripened and fallen, its job is to decompose and become the fertile soil for the seeds of enlightenment held within it.

BITTERNESS TURNS INTO RIPENESS

FINDING THE QUALITIES UNDERNEATH OUR FOIBLES

A person's weaknesses are only his or her strengths out of balance. An assertive personality out of balance becomes dominant. A yielding personality out of balance becomes a "doormat." A confident person out of balance becomes arrogant. A humble person out of balance becomes self-deprecating.

Examine your personality and become aware of a fault or foible you would like to transform. Then ask yourself

"What is the quality that is out of balance here? How can I transform this weakness into a strength?"

When you next find yourself exhibiting the negative personality trait that you are working on, remember that it is not a permanent flaw in your nature but only a potential quality that is temporarily out of balance. Then try to correct your behavior as you feel appropriate.

FIND OUT WHICH QUALITIES ARE OUT OF BALANCE

❝ People should think less about what they ought to do and more about what they ought to be. ❞

MEISTER ECKHART
CHRISTIAN MYSTIC

❝ As the light grows, we see issuing from our heart a whole swarm of shameful feelings, like filthy reptiles crawling from a hidden cave. But we are not worse than we were. On the contrary we are better. But while our faults diminish, the light we see them by waxes brighter. ❞

FÉNELON
CHRISTIAN MYSTIC

Grace and effort

MANY SPIRITUAL TRADITIONS *teach we must master the lower self through discipline and effort. In the Zen tradition the wayward ego-self is pictured like a wild bull that must be tamed through perseverance in spiritual practice. While most of us are slaves to our own passions and desires, the spiritual masters have mastered their own egos. They are no longer dominated by its every whim and fancy, but are self-controlled and so more able to be selfless.*

TAME THE BULL

*PARADOXICALLY, PRAYING IS MAKING
THE EFFORT TO ASK FOR GRACE*

PICKING YOURSELF UP BY YOUR BOOTSTRAPS

Other traditions teach that enlightenment comes only through realizing that we are helpless and must rely on divine grace. They argue that if we seek to overcome our self through our own will we are, in effect, trying to "pick ourselves up by our own bootstraps." How can the self master the self? If we believe we are the "doer" making the effort to be self-disciplined, how will we come to understand that there is no separate self to be self-disciplined or otherwise?

EFFORT IS GRACE

Although these two approaches may seem contradictory, they are actually two sides of a spiritual paradox. Spiritual practices cannot force or guarantee realization, they can only create conditions conducive to the experience of enlightenment spontaneously occurring. And picturing ourselves as helplessly calling on the grace of a Higher Power is actually an act of personal will that tricks the ego into giving up its claims to personal power. From an enlightened perspective they are indistinguishable. Any effort we may think we are making is in fact God's grace, and any grace that we believe to be coming from an external source is in reality coming from our true Self. Most spiritual traditions teach a combination of personal effort and reliance on God's grace.

Self-Discipline and Spontaneity

Self-discipline is about setting up good habits so that you automatically function in ways that are helpful to your spiritual growth. Most of us do not have to think about basic personal hygiene because we were trained as children to clean ourselves each day. Developing spiritual self-discipline is about similarly training ourselves to attend to our psychological hygiene. We would not dream of going out in the morning unwashed from the night before and subjecting other people to our unpleasant body odors. Similarly, we need to develop the habit of regular spiritual practice so that we clean our inner self and do not subject others to our unpleasant personality traits.

However, while some spiritual masters recommend strict self-discipline, others encourage us to be completely spontaneous; to respond naturally to the immediacy of the moment; to let the spirit blow through us like the wind, taking us where it wills. As Jesus teaches in the Gospel of John:

"The wind blows where it will and you hear the sound of it, but you don't know where it comes from or where it goes; it is the same with everyone born of the spirit."

When we are spontaneous we are free from the illusion that we are leading our lives, and instead allow our lives to lead us. Many spiritual masters teach that, while self-discipline is an important stage on the journey of awakening, ultimately only completely "letting go" opens us up to the experience of enlightenment. Enlightenment cannot be forced, so all that we can do is avoid getting in the way of it naturally happening.

As the anonymous author of a Christian mystical text called "The Cloud of Unknowing" explains, enlightenment is "an impromptu and unpremeditated impulse, which leaps up to God as a spark springs from the coal."

BE SPONTANEOUS!

SUSTAINING A REGULAR SPIRITUAL PRACTICE

The key to sustaining a regular spiritual practice is motivation. You really have to want to adopt such a regime. If you do not, or if you only feel you *should* undertake such a discipline, then this way is probably not for you.

If you do have the desire, the next most important thing is not to be too ambitious initially. You may be able to sustain a regular spiritual practice of an hour morning and night for a few days, but soon this may become too much and you will abandon it. Better to start with making fewer demands and surprising yourself by your success than being too demanding and ending up disappointed.

Dealing with failure is the next important hurdle. Use your failure as a spiritual practice in itself, not as an excuse to abandon your practice. See it as an opportunity simply to start afresh, without guilt or recrimination.

A good way to develop a regular spiritual practice is to state clearly your intentions for one week – it may be best to write them down so that you can be absolutely sure of what you have decided. For example, you may decide to meditate every night for 20 minutes before sleeping. Once you have decided what you are going to do, make sure you practice, even if you are so drowsy that you keep nodding off. Do it whatever, even if you are getting nothing from the practice. Then at the end of the week evaluate what you have been doing and alter your practice as appropriate. Eventually you will settle down into a routine that works for you and that you are able to follow effortlessly as an integral part of your way of life.

> 66 A minute of meditation is a minute of peace and happiness. If meditation is not pleasant for you, you are not practicing correctly. 99

THICH NHAT HANH
ZEN MASTER AND POET WHO WAS
NOMINATED FOR THE NOBEL PEACE
PRIZE BY MARTIN LUTHER KING

THICH NHAT HANH

This week I will start each day with 6 salutes to the sun and meditate for 20 minutes before going to sleep

“ You must be lamps unto yourselves.
Rely on yourselves and do not rely on external help. ”

BUDDHA

෴

“ The wind of grace is always blowing
and we must align our sail with it. ”

KABIR
HINDU SAINT

THE BUDDHA BY ODILON REDON

Morality

FROM A SOCIAL PERSPECTIVE, *morality is a set of rules that help people live together in harmony. For those on the spiritual path, however, morality is not about slavishly obeying preordained rules of conduct. It is about nurturing a spiritual state of awareness from which we naturally act well. Different traditions present us with different moral guidelines to assist us in our spiritual awakening. At the heart of all of them, however, is a universal principle of reciprocity that encourages us to treat others as we would ourselves wish to be treated.*

LEARNING TO LIVE TOGETHER

THE ETHIC OF EMPATHY

We are all conscious beings who experience joy and pain, who act well and who make mistakes, who are struggling to make sense of a crazy world, and who are sometimes overwhelmed by their own selfishness. If we can see others as essentially identical to ourselves, it opens the possibility of loving others as ourselves; of treating others as we ourselves long to be treated, with understanding, care, forgiveness, and kindness.

NATURAL MORALITY

The masters teach "love others as yourself" not only because this is necessary for social cohesion, but because it reveals the profound mystic truth that we are all One. We are being taught to "love others as other aspects of the One Self." When we know that we are intimately connected to all other beings, acting well toward others is as obvious and spontaneous as our left hand assisting our right hand. We don't need to be told or cajoled into good behavior. When we experience ourselves as expressions of the One, we discover we are goodness itself. The moral codes taught by the great sages are techniques to cultivate this natural morality by helping us transcend habitual preoccupations with our own self.

Living a Whole-some Life

Walking the spiritual path brings us closer to God, who is all goodness. Indeed, our word "God" is derived from a Germanic source meaning "The Good." A selfish action, of whatever form, seeks to benefit the "part" without regard for the "Whole." It is therefore not "whole-some," "good," or "Godly." A "whole-some" action, on the other hand, is one that is done with the intention of benefiting the Whole. It is in harmony with the Tao. It is following the will of God.

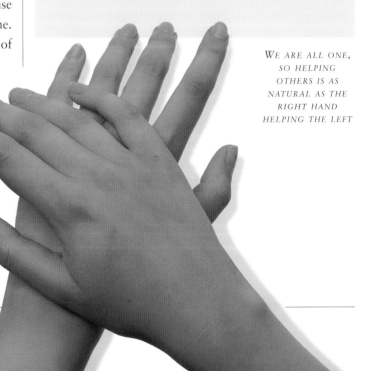

WE ARE ALL ONE, SO HELPING OTHERS IS AS NATURAL AS THE RIGHT HAND HELPING THE LEFT

THE UNIVERSAL PRINCIPLE OF RECIPROCITY

" Treat others as you would be treated. "

JESUS
GOSPEL OF MATTHEW

❧❧❧❧

" Not one of you is a believer until he loves
for his brother what he loves for himself. "

HADITH
ISLAMIC SCRIPTURE

❧❧❧❧

" Do not afflict others with anything that you
yourself would not wish to suffer. "

EPICTETUS
CYNIC PHILOSOPHER

❧❧❧❧

" Try your best to treat others as you would
be treated, and you will find that this is the
shortest way to goodness. "

MENCIUS
CONFUCIAN SAGE

❧❧❧❧

" A man should go about treating
all creatures as he himself would like
to be treated. "

SUTRAKRITANGA
JAIN SCRIPTURE

" One should not behave toward others in
anyway that is disagreeable to oneself. This is the
essence of morality. All other activities are due to
selfish desire. "

MAHABHARATA
HINDU SCRIPTURE

❧❧❧❧

" Such as you wish your neighbor to be to you,
such also be to your neighbors. "

SEXTUS
PYTHAGOREAN PHILOSOPHER

❧❧❧❧

" Act not to others in ways you yourself
would find hurtful. "

UDANA-VARGA
BUDDHIST SCRIPTURE

❧❧❧❧

" That nature only is good when it does not unto
another whatever is not good for itself. "

DADISTAN-I-DINIK
ZOROASTRIAN SCRIPTURE

❧❧❧❧

" What is hateful to you, do not do to your
neighbor. This is the whole of the Law. The rest is
only commentary on this. Go and learn. "

TALMUD
JEWISH SCRIPTURE

Zen Master Ikkyu

Ikkyu, who called himself "Crazy Cloud," is one of the most outrageous and best loved of the Zen masters. He believed Zen was about becoming a natural human being who enjoyed life to the full, and thought a puritan saint was nowhere near a Buddha. He taught that instead of endlessly studying Buddhist scriptures, we should learn to read the love letters sent by the snow, the wind, and the rain. He burned his copies of the scriptures and followed the dictates of his intuition. He simply expressed his own nature – which included spending time with pleasure girls in brothels!

Having lived the life of a tramp for most of his days, Ikkyu became an abbot of an important Zen temple. Just before his death he foretold that some of his students would become hermits in the mountains, devoted to their spiritual practices, while others would drink wine and frequent brothels. He himself had followed both of these lifestyles and regarded both of them as good ways to practice Zen. His only wish was that none of his students should became professional Zen priests babbling on about Buddhism. This would be anti-Zen.

CULTIVATING EMPATHY

Spiritual ethics are based on empathy. Today as you go about your daily life, make space in your awareness to empathize with others. Ask yourself how it must feel to be in their positions. Don't just accept a superficial response to this question. Use the power of your imagination to understand as much about their predicaments as you can.

You may like to try this with someone who is irritating you at work, or someone you usually ignore such as a down-and-out begging on a street corner, or someone who has an opposing view on life to yourself.

Having opened your heart, allow any actions that may be appropriate to spring naturally and spontaneously from your sense of empathy.

66 Duty without love is deplorable.

Duty with love is desirable.

Love without duty is divine. 99

SAI BABA
HINDU GURU

❧❧❧❧

66 Playing at love in the summer house,
a beautiful young girl and an old Zen monk;
passionate embraces and affectionate kisses –
this doesn't feel like hell to me! 99

IKKYU
ZEN MASTER

66 God inhabits every soul, even those
of the greatest sinners in the world. 99

ST. JOHN OF THE CROSS
CHRISTIAN MYSTIC

❧❧❧❧

66 I have seen the One who is, and how He
is the being of all creatures. God is present in
everything that exists, in a devil and a good
angel, in heaven and hell, in good deeds and
in adultery and murder, in the beautiful and
the ugly. Therefore, while I am in this Truth,
I take as much delight in seeing and
understanding his presence in a devil and the
act of adultery as I do in an angel and a
good deed. 99

ANGELA OF FOLIGNO
CHRISTIAN MYSTIC

LATIN BIBLE

Humility

*A*LL SPIRITUAL TRADITIONS *emphasize the importance of humility. Humility is about acknowledging our personal insignificance before the awesome majesty of Life. As the Christian saint Diadochos of Photiki teaches, "Humility unites humanity with God." It helps us see the ego-self for what it is – a small part of a much greater Whole. The Taoist sage Lao Tzu points out that it is only because the ocean is lower than all rivers that it is the greatest body of water. If we wish to become one with the ocean of Tao we must, likewise, become humble and lowly.*

LAO TZU
ON HIS OX

ESSENTIAL EQUALITY

Most of us unconsciously divide people up into three categories: those we look up to as being better than us in some way, those we treat as equals, and those we look down on as being lesser. People are indeed better and worse in myriad ways. Some are clever and others are stupid. Some are beautiful and others ugly. Some are compassionate and others selfish. Humility is about focusing on the one important respect in which we are all completely equal. Each one of us is a conscious witness of the unfolding mystery of life.

NO ONE SPECIAL

Humility is not wishing to appear special, because that would make someone else seem mediocre. But humility is not about depreciating ourselves and inflating others. It is about simply ceasing to be a separate self competing for importance and attention with millions of other separate selves. Instead it is valuing ourselves as an aspect of the One Universal Self and so also honoring and appreciating all the beings who are its other expressions. It is not about putting ourselves down, it is about lifting ourselves up. It is acknowledging our ego-self to be far less than it would like, but our deeper nature to be more than we can imagine.

EQUAL PARTS OF THE WHOLE

Humility is an important spiritual quality that can be constantly cultivated in our daily lives. Watch out for when you unconsciously dismiss someone else as lesser than you. Then remember that, although your outer forms may be different, your inner essence is identical. You are both expressions of the One Consciousness of the universe.

Ironically, it is our own sense of inadequacy that causes us to puff ourselves up or put someone else down. When your feel you are lacking in humility, instead of giving yourself a hard time about it, try reassuring yourself about your own worth. This will allow you to feel more generous in valuing others.

“ Whoever exalts himself
will be humbled.
Whoever humbles himself
will be exalted. ”

JESUS
GOSPEL OF MATTHEW

❦❦❦

“ The tall tower of virtue cannot stand long unless it
is based on the low foundation of humility. ”

THOMAS À KEMPIS
CHRISTIAN SAINT

*WE ARE ALL UNIQUE
EXPRESSIONS OF ONE
CONSCIOUSNESS*

Acceptance

SPIRITUALITY TEACHES US to cultivate a state of complete acceptance: for only if we accept whatever happens to us in our lives as the will of God, will we give up our own personal agenda and transcend the separate self. When we divide our experiences up into good and bad, pleasant and unpleasant, desirable and undesirable, these value judgments trap us in duality. Acceptance allows us to glimpse the Oneness of Life. To see things as they are we must let things be as they are. Zen master Seng-t'san teaches, "The Way is easy for those who have no preferences!"

LET THINGS BE

GOOD AND BAD IN EVERYTHING

Those things we call "good" we find easy to accept, but those things we call "bad" we do not. Spirituality, however, teaches that such judgements are purely subjective and superficial. What is good for us may be bad for others and vice versa. What seems bad to us today may seem beneficial some time later. Good and bad are not as distinct and definable as we may believe. There is nothing so bad that good cannot come from it and nothing so good that bad cannot come from it. Even the worst of situations has the potential to leave us richer by helping us grow in courage, faith, and perseverance. Even the best situation can leave us feeling poorer and bereft because it will inevitably pass away. Every situation is both good and bad. There is always something we like and something we don't like about our lives. When we understand this we are able to accept the apparent imperfections of life as part of the wider picture.

ACCEPTANCE NOT APATHY

But acceptance is not the same thing as resignation or an apathetic abdication of involvement with life. It is refusing to get consumed by how we would like things to be and instead actively engaging with the reality that confronts us. Acceptance is not passively putting up with life – some things are simply unacceptable. Our feelings of discontent and our desire for change also need to be accepted. Acceptance is about fully embracing life as it is – struggles and all.

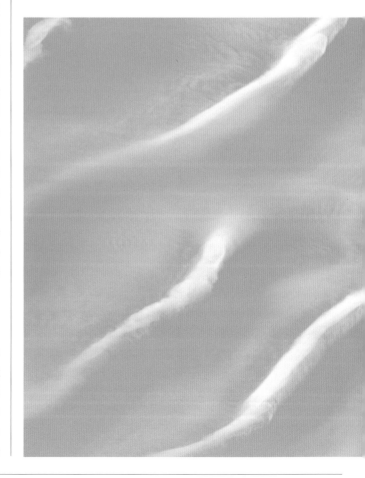

Accepting Our Fate
but Transforming Ourselves

The ancient Pagan philosopher Epictetus taught that happiness comes from understanding the basic principle that some things are within our control and other things simply have to be accepted. Although we cannot chose what happens to us, we can choose how we respond. If we accept our fate while also seeking to transform ourselves, we will find peace and contentment. Epictetus explains:

"Our opinions, ambitions, desires, and aversions are in our control. We can change the contents of our inner character. Our body, wealth, fame, and social status are not in our control. They are external to us and not our concern."

What Is Good and
What Is Bad?

Once upon a time an old farmer lost his best stallion. His neighbor came around that evening to express his condolences, but the old farmer just said, "Who knows what is good and what is bad?" The next day the stallion returned bringing with him three wild mares. The neighbor rushed around to celebrate, but the old farmer simply said, "Who knows what is good and what is bad?" The following day the farmer's son fell from one of the wild mares while trying to break her in and broke his leg. The neighbor turned up to make sure all was well, but the old farmer just said, "Who knows what is good and what is bad?" The next day the army came to conscript the farmer's son to go and fight in the wars, but finding him an invalid left him with his father. The neighbor thought to himself, "Who knows what is good and what is bad?"

TAOIST TEACHING STORY

EVERYTHING TEMPORAL PASSES AWAY

REDEEMING THE PAST

Spirituality teaches us to avoid judging everything that happens to us as "good" or "bad," but to accept what is and find the goodness in it. This can often be very difficult. This exercise helps us learn to accept the present by redeeming the past.

It encourages us to consider the goodness in past events that we previously dismissed as bad. If the things we thought were "bad" in the past, we can now see were actually good in ways we did not appreciate at the time, then we can begin to see that what seem like present misfortunes may turn out to have played some valuable role in our lives. It reminds us to trust that, sooner or later, we will understand why what is happening is happening and where it is taking us.

✺ Review events in your past that at the time you deemed to be bad.

✺ Dwell on these events and consider if, in some unexpected way, something good has come out of them.

✺ Did your misfortune show you something about yourself or the world you live in?

✺ Did it help you grow in some way?

✺ Did you learn something valuable from it?

✺ If not, can you learn something from it now?

My mother dying was one of the worst things that ever happened to me, but it did lead to my sister and I talking together at the funeral for the first time in six years. I felt really bad that it took something as bad as mum dying to get us back together again after what was just a stupid squabble, but I guess I was forced to see just how stubborn I can be. Ever since we have been completely there for each other – I feel like healing our relationship was mum's last gift to us.

“ Whenever adversity comes his way, regardless of what it is, who it comes from, and how frequently, the truly patient person accepts everything as coming from the hand of God. ”

THOMAS À KEMPIS
CHRISTIAN SAINT

✺✺✺✺

“ What is called good is perfect and what is called bad is just as perfect. ”

WALT WHITMAN
MYSTICAL POET

✺✺✺✺

“ Humans see some deeds as good and others as evil, but our Lord doesn't see things like this; for everything is given its nature by God and so all that is done is done by God. There is no doer but Him. ”

MOTHER JULIAN OF NORWICH
CHRISTIAN MYSTIC

BUDDHA

Forgiveness

*S*PIRITUALITY TEACHES THAT *life is a process of gradually expanding our awareness. We do not start out enlightened but rather as confused and egocentric, so it is inevitable that we will all make many mistakes. The saints and sages, therefore, urge us not to judge others for their mistakes, but to reach out with forgiveness. Forgiveness is an act of great generosity. It is understanding someone even when we have every right to condemn that person. It is loving someone even when he or she is being unlovable. It is accepting the unacceptable.*

ST. BASIL

WHEN WE JUDGE WE ARE CONDEMNED

The Hindu guru Sai Baba teaches, "Do not judge others, for when another is judged you yourself are condemned." This is because when we blame another we not only exile that person from our heart, but at the same time cut ourselves off from a part of the Whole. Forgiveness not only unites us with those from whom we have been divided, but also with the Higher Power. God forgives all of us because God is unconditional love. To know this uniting love, we too must forgive all those who have wronged us.

FORGIVENESS IS NATURAL

The Talmud, a Jewish scripture, teaches, "He who takes vengeance or bears a grudge acts like one who, having cut one hand while handling a knife, avenges himself by stabbing the other hand." We are all One, and seeking to avenge one wrong by committing another is like hurting ourselves twice. When we know we are all One, vengeance is ridiculous and forgiveness is natural.

NO ONE TO BLAME

From an enlightened perspective blame is always inappropriate, because there are no separate selves to be condemned. All is One, and the deeds of every individual are simply an expression of this Oneness. The enlightened masters have transcended all judgments because they have understood there is no one to judge.

Learning to Forgive

We find it easy to forgive children because we understand that behaving badly is an inevitable part of the process of learning to act well. The saints and sages show the same compassionate tolerance toward everyone.

Love Your Enemies

In the Gospel of Matthew, Jesus teaches:

"Love your enemies and pray for those who persecute you, so that you may be sons of your Heavenly Father. For he makes the sun rise on evil men as well as good men; and sends the rains to unjust men as well as just men."

We are not being asked to "like" our enemies or to approve of what they do, but to love them; to sense the underlying Oneness of which we are all a part; to see our enemies not as intrinsically bad and unlovable, but as tragically trapped in their separateness and suffering through their selfishness. If we meet evil with evil, then things can only get worse; but if we meet evil with goodness, then the situation may miraculously be transformed for the better.

Pray for Your Enemies

The Christian hermit Abba Zeno teaches that we should make a priority of praying for our enemies as a way of opening ourselves to God who is all-loving and all-forgiving:

"If someone wants to be heard by God, then before he prays for his own soul, or for anything else, let him pray with all his heart for his enemies. If he does this, God will hear everything he asks."

The Christian mystic William Law, likewise, teaches that a simple way of healing the divisions between ourselves and those we have exiled from our heart is to pray to the Higher Power for their well-being:

"You cannot possibly have any ill-temper, or show any unkind behavior to a man for whose welfare you are so much concerned, as to be his advocate with God in private. For you cannot possibly despise and ridicule that man whom your private prayers recommend to the love and favor of God."

THE CRUCIFIXION, PAINTED BY ODILON REDON

OPENING THE HEART AND FORGIVING

Is there someone you are blaming for something and need to forgive? If so, this visualization exercise will help you embrace that person with loving acceptance.

1 *Sit in meditation and bring the person you need to forgive to mind.*

2 *Imagine taking him or her by the hand and walking together into a radiant bright light.*

3 *Feel the light as a love that embraces everyone and everything irrespective of worth, just as the sun shines on the good and bad alike.*

4 *Once in the light, offer up a prayer for that person's well-being to the Higher Power.*

When you next meet that person, bring to mind the image of both of you together in the light and allow yourself intuitively to say and do whatever is appropriate.

WHEN FORGIVENESS IS REFUSED

It is difficult to forgive people who are so embroiled with the ego-self that they cannot accept your forgiveness. If you encounter this dilemma, this visualization exercise can help you understand that such people cannot respond to your forgiveness because they are too frightened to open their hearts.

1 *Imagine this person's soul as a little innocent child trapped inside the cage of its separate self.*

2 *Focus on that soul and imagine it calling out beyond the mask of its dysfunctional personality, begging you to help it escape.*

3 *Understand that every time you react to the hostility of that personality, the voice of the little child gets fainter as it fades away into the distance; and every time you ignore the superficial ego, the greater the chance of the soul escaping from its prison.*

Next time you meet this person, concentrate on opening your heart with love and acceptance, and in so doing give him or her the opportunity suddenly to break free.

❝ Where there is forgiveness, there is God Himself. ❞

ADI GRANTH
SIKH SCRIPTURE

❝ My detractors are actually good friends, because, if I am equanimous and accepting, the power of love and humility, which is born of the Unborn, grows within me. ❞

YUNG-CHIA TA-SHIH
ZEN MASTER

❝ This is the philosopher's way; to be flogged like an ass and to love those who beat him, to be father and brother of all humanity. ❞

EPICTETUS
PAGAN PHILOSOPHER

❝ A superior being does not render evil for evil. A noble soul will ever exercise compassion even toward those who enjoy injuring others. ❞

RAMAYANA
HINDU SCRIPTURE

LAO TZU

Positivity

*I*T CAN SOUND LIKE *a bland truism, but whether life seems good or bad depends on whether we think it is good or bad. Nothing is negative or positive in itself – only thinking makes it so. As our thoughts about an event change, so do our positive or negative feelings toward it. The memory of a wonderful wedding day changes after the later experience of a traumatic divorce. The week that everything went wrong for us becomes, in time, the source of our funniest anecdotes.*

A THRILLING ADVENTURE

How the world appears to us is a result of how we see it Based on this understanding, spirituality encourages us to view life in a positive light. To make the most of all it offers. To avoid getting bogged down in depression and disappointment. If we are positive, we are often able to find ways to turn around "negative" situations that we would not have recognized if we were too busy getting depressed. With a positive attitude anything can be embraced as part of the adventure of life. In his seventies, the psychedelic drugs guru Timothy Leary, refusing to see the onset of dementia as something negative, quipped, "Senility is wasted on the old. For me it's a thrilling adventure."

CRISIS

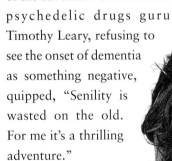

TIMOTHY LEARY

CRISIS OR OPPORTUNITY?

It is interesting that the Chinese character meaning "crisis" also means "opportunity." Seen from a positive perspective, the catastrophes of our lives are also our greatest opportunities for transformation. An "emergency" is a chance to "emerge" from our preconceptions of how life is and who we are – forcing us to look again and discover new ways of being. Approached in a positive spirit, it is when our life breaks down that we have the opportunity to break through to another level of awareness.

FAITH

Many spiritual traditions use the word "faith" to describe the state of positive acceptance that allows us to enter unreservedly into the dramas of life without being overwhelmed by fear. Faith is sometimes interpreted as unquestioning belief in religious dogmas. But this is a very superficial understanding. Faith is trusting in the essential goodness of life, even when times are bad. Faith is having confidence in the meaningfulness of events that may seem meaningless. Faith is remembering our transcendental experiences when we come down to earth with a bang. Faith is not disregarding our deepest insights when we no longer feel inspired. Faith is not forgetting God just because we temporarily do not feel the Presence. Faith is confidence in the way it is.

AFFIRMATIONS

Affirmations are a technique used in the New Age movement to assist personal transformation by reprogramming oneself through positive thinking. You can repeat an affirmation to yourself in meditation or while you are driving or going about your daily life. You could also try writing down your affirmation over and over again.

Choose an affirmation that contradicts a negative self-image that you wish to transform. If you think of yourself as lethargic, for example, take as your affirmation "I am vibrant and full of positive energy," or if you see yourself as selfish try "I am full of abundant love and naturally giving," and so forth. Make your affirmation positive. Don't say "I am not ..." but affirm "I am ..."

66 We are what we think.

All that we are arises with our thoughts.

With our thoughts we create the world. 99

THE BUDDHA

66 Faith is the bird that feels the light

when the dawn is still dark. 99

RABINDRANATH TAGORE
HINDU SAGE

Appreciation

THE CHRISTIAN SAGE *Meister Eckhart teaches, "If the only prayer you say in your whole life is 'thank you,' that would be enough." Spirituality encourages us to cultivate a heartfelt appreciation of life. A "Big Yes" in response to all the joys that we delight in and sorrows we endure. A deep gratitude for being here at all. A Zen master was once asked how he had achieved enlightenment. He replied, "By simply being grateful for everything that happens." Don't wait until you are dying before you realize how much you love your life.*

thank you!

APPRECIATE THE GIFT OF LIFE

EVERY DAY IS A GOOD DAY

There is a Zen saying "Every day is a good day." By adopting an appreciative attitude, we can let each day be good in its own way. It may be good because it is easy and enjoyable or because it is a challenge that reveals our present spiritual limitations. Every experience can be appreciated when it is understood in the context of the whole life process. Without the death and decay of autumn and winter there could not be the growth and flowering of spring and summer. All the seasons play their part and can be appreciated for making the whole cycle of the year possible. Likewise, those experiences we call "bad" as well as those we think of as "good" can be appreciated as playing an integral part in the unfolding of our lives.

SWIMMING IN AN OCEAN OF GOD

It is easy to forget how much we are given every moment, just to sustain this remarkable existence we so often take for granted. Surrounded as we are by life's bounty, it is incredible that we ever feel impoverished. Zen master Hsueh-feng laughs, "Immersed in water, you stretch out your hands for a drink." The Hindu guru Sai Baba declares, "You are a fish swimming in an ocean of God."

IT'S A WONDERFUL WORLD

THE BIG THANK YOU

Being appreciative is so simple, yet it can completely transform our lives. Experiment with unconditionally appreciating yourself, others, and all that happens to you.

Are you so busy wanting more that you are missing what you've got? Appreciate all the wonders in your life. Feel how thankful you are for your loved ones, your opportunities, health, wealth, the sun that shines and the air you breath, the fact that you are alive at all. They are all only temporary gifts, so fully appreciate them now while you have the chance.

See every experience as a valuable gift. Some gifts are pleasant and to be enjoyed. Some gifts are challenges that can help your spiritual evolution. See the good in every experience, and every experience will become a good experience.

Wonder of Wonders

Student
"Is there anything more miraculous than the wonders of nature?"

Zen master
"Yes. Your appreciation of these wonders."

❝ Even if every hair on my head
could say 'thank you,'
I would be unable to
express my gratitude. ❞

JALAL AL-DIN RUMI
SUFI SAGE

Beyond concepts

CHILDREN LIVE IN *the mystery of existence because they have no concepts to describe what is happening to them. The price they pay, however, is that they find it very difficult to function in the world and rely on adults to take care of them. As we grow up we construct an ever more complex conceptual picture of the world, which enables us to function within it. But the price we pay is that we believe this conceptual map is reality. We begin to think we know how things are and lose our sense of wonder and mystery. Spirituality is about retaining the wonder of childhood while cultivating the wisdom of age.*

LEARNING CONCEPTS

STATUE OF THE BUDDHA IN UTTAR PRADESH, INDIA

ACKNOWLEDGING OUR IGNORANCE

Spirituality is not about returning to the helpless state of being an infant, but it is about remembering that life essentially remains as much of a profound mystery as it was when we were too young even to think. To regain this primal sense of wonder, the saints and sages urge us to acknowledge our essential ignorance, to realize that even our most cherished beliefs are just opinions. They are not encouraging us to become fools but to see things as they are. Concepts are just concepts. The Truth cannot be expressed by ideas.

KNOWING NOTHING

Rather than building our lives on the rickety foundation of a hodgepodge of personal prejudices, the spiritual masters recommend cultivating an attitude of "don't know." The ancient Pagan Oracle at Delphi decreed that the philosopher Socrates was the wisest man in the world because he alone knew that he knew nothing. Spirituality is very ironic. We set out on the spiritual path wanting to know the Truth, but the Truth is we don't know anything. We begin feeling troubled by the fact that life doesn't make sense, but we end up realizing that our problem was the answer. Life doesn't make sense. How could it? How could the limited intellect ever comprehend the infinite grandeur of the cosmos and the unfathomable mystery of Being? As the Christian mystic Angela of Foligno says:

"The joy of the saints is the joy of incomprehension. They understand that they cannot possibly understand."

EXPLANATIONS ARE NOT THE TRUTH

Spirituality is not about acquiring more and more profound ideas. Instead, it is about discovering the source of all ideas. Ideas are like clouds passing across the empty blue sky of Consciousness. All ideas, even profound spiritual ideas, clutter up Consciousness and distract us from an awareness of Awareness itself. The Buddhist sage Milarepa teaches:

"Even a desire for more instruction is a distraction. Too many explanations without the essence is like an orchard of trees without fruit. Knowing many explanations is not knowing the Truth. Too much conceptualization has no spiritual benefit. Only the secret treasure benefits the heart. If you want riches, concentrate on this."

INTELLECTUAL UNDERSTANDING

There is a constant danger that we mistake intellectual understanding for experiential realization. Just as saying the word "food" will never feed us, intellectual understanding will never satisfy our need for meaning. Spiritual philosophy can only help us escape from the stranglehold of conventional concepts that are limiting our perception of the miracle of life. In themselves spiritual ideas are just more concepts. If we hold on to them too tightly, they are just as limiting as any other concepts. The Buddhist sage Nagarjuna teaches bluntly:

"All philosophies are mental fabrications. There has never been a single doctrine by which one could enter the true essence of things."

INTUITIVE UNDERSTANDING

Ultimately, spirituality teaches that the answers we are seeking are found by letting go of our questions and sinking into a deep inner silence. Spirituality does not resolve our dilemmas with definitive answers, it dissolves them into an innate intuitive understanding entirely beyond the scope of words ever to express. As the Zen master Daie explains:

"The teachings expounded in all the scriptures are merely commentaries on the spontaneous cry – 'Ah, this!'"

ART COMMUNICATES WITHOUT WORDS

LOOK AT THE MOON, NOT THE FINGER

A Finger Pointing at the Moon

Spirituality is not about grasping a complex philosophy. Spiritual ideas point beyond themselves to an immediate experience of Reality. Zen teachings are often compared to a finger pointing at the moon. The finger is not the moon and the teachings are not the Truth. Indeed, to see the moon we must stop looking at the pointing finger.

A Raft to the Farther Shore

A clear idea is like a window through which we can glimpse Reality. But to reach Reality we must open the inner door of Consciousness and walk through. We then have no need of a window. The Buddha compared his teachings to a raft to carry his students to the farther shore of enlightenment. Having arrived, what use is a raft? Ideas can be very useful on the spiritual journey, but to arrive they must be abandoned. If we never disembark from the raft we will be forever at sea.

LIVING WITH "DON'T KNOW"

Spirituality teaches us to see all our ideas, no matter how elevated, as just opinions that are at best only relatively true. Sit quietly and bring to mind some of your most cherished spiritual ideas.

Explore your relationship to them. Are you reluctant to consider them as mere opinions? Have you bound yourself so tightly to them that they are incapable of performing their real role of releasing you into a non-conceptual direct experience of the Truth?

If you find yourself unwilling to see the relative nature of your beliefs, you have made a valuable discovery. Focus on these beliefs and try to understand what it is about them that makes you so attached to them. If you can, let them go and dissolve the mind into the emptiness of "don't know."

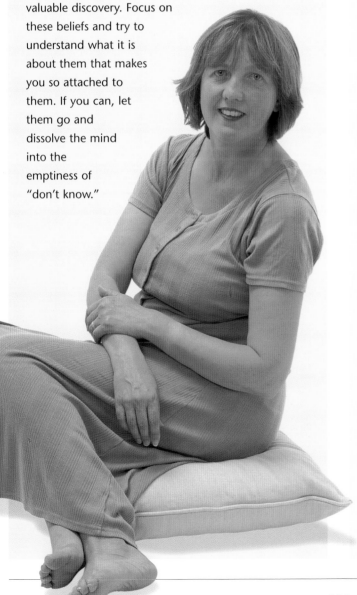

> Unless you return to being like children, you will never enter the kingdom of heaven.

JESUS
GOSPEL OF MATTHEW

> The wise man, established in the Self, lives like a child.

ASHTAVAKRA GITA
HINDU SCRIPTURE

> As long as there is a 'who' asking the questions, that 'who' will continue to remain puzzled.

RAMESH BALSEKAR
HINDU SAGE

> Do not search for truth. Just stop having opinions.

SENG T'SAN
ZEN MASTER

A MONK CONTEMPLATES

Suffering

T IS FUNDAMENTAL to human nature that we wish to be happy and to avoid suffering. Yet suffering in some shape or form seems to be unavoidable. Sooner or later each one of us is forced to endure grief, pain, melancholy, and disappointment. Must life involve suffering and, if so, why? If the Higher Power is good and loving, why does it countenance the horrible afflictions that sometimes burden us? Can suffering be avoided? And if so, how?

IS GRIEF UNAVOIDABLE?

SUFFERING IS SELF-CREATED

Spirituality teaches that suffering is not the same thing as pain or grief or failure. Suffering is how we react to events that happen to us. Suffering is self-created. It is our inability to accept experiences that seem to be against our self-interest. Suffering is the price of believing ourselves to be a mortal body and personality. The more we identify with the separate self, the more we suffer. The more we understand our essential nature to be the witnessing Consciousness, the less we suffer. Suffering, therefore, is one of our teachers on the spiritual path who reveals where we are holding tightly to the illusion of separateness.

SUFFERING EVOKES LOVE

Although this is a powerful way of looking at suffering, it can seem inadequate in the face of the awful intensity and immediacy of the actual experience itself. Indeed, if it were not for suffering it would be easy to rest content with a philosophical understanding of life without ever opening the heart. But no spiritual philosophy can truly mitigate the horrors of the holocaust or the sight of a loved one in anguish. Suffering forces us to reach beyond an intellectual understanding of spirituality to the experience of love. Only the power of love can transform suffering into something meaningful, bringing poignancy, togetherness, and courage to warm the chilling futility of pain and despair.

HIROSHIMA AFTER THE ATOM BOMB

The Buddha's Quest

The Buddha was born a wealthy prince and was deliberately sheltered from all forms of human affliction. When he finally discovered the horrors of illness, old age, and death, he was so deeply moved that he abandoned his luxurious lifestyle and decided he would not rest until he found a way to free humanity from suffering. Eventually, while in deep meditation, he became enlightened and found the answer. He did not discover how magically to change the outer world and eliminate poverty, illness, and death. He realized that we could change the private world of the mind and eliminate suffering from the inside.

66 All the terrible calamities of the world are born of egoism. When I am under the influence of egoism I suffer. When I am free from egoism I am happy. 99

VASISHTHA
HINDU YOGI

A Nepalese Buddha

All of Life Is Suffering

The Buddha presented his solution to the pressing human dilemma of how to deal with sufferings in the form of "The Four Noble Truths." The first of these was a blunt statement of the extent of the problem: "All of life is suffering." This may seem overly pessimistic, but the Buddha understood that we inhabit three basic states, all of which entail suffering. Not getting what we desire, getting what we don't desire, and getting what we desire but knowing that everything is impermanent and we will inevitably lose the object of our desire.

Selfishness Causes Suffering

From this the Buddha concluded the second of the Four Noble Truths: "The origin of suffering is selfish desire and attachment." We suffer because we want things to be other than they are. We want life to be arranged in such a way that it serves the interests of the separate self that we mistakenly presume ourselves to be. From this the Buddha concluded the third of the Four Noble Truths: "There is a way to stop suffering." If selfish desire is the problem, then its eradication is the solution. Thus the fourth Noble Truth proclaims, "This way is the Eightfold Path: right understanding; right thinking; right speech; right attitude; right livelihood; right effort; right mindfulness; right concentration." If we cultivate these qualities, we eradicate our self-orientation and transcend suffering.

The Buddha's Four Noble Truths

First Truth
All of life is suffering.

Second Truth
The origin of suffering is selfish desire and attachment.

Third Truth
There is a way to stop suffering.

Fourth Truth
This way is the Eightfold Path:
- Right understanding
- Right thinking
- Right speech
- Right attitude
- Right livelihood
- Right effort
- Right mindfulness
- Right concentration

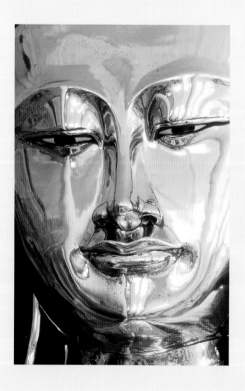

PILGRIMS PROSTRATE THEMSELVES AT A MONASTERY IN TIBET

Suffering Willingly

Suffering is a powerful initiation. In many traditions pilgrims deliberately court suffering so that they can learn endurance and transcendence. By suffering willingly, suffering is conquered. These teachings are powerfully represented by the Christian crucifix – a portrayal of a dying man being tortured in the most awful of ways and yet triumphant over death.

WORKING WITH SUFFERING

Spirituality teaches that suffering is an important part of the journey of life. It is not something to be escaped or suppressed, but fully experienced, understood, and passed beyond. When you are suffering, in whatever way, you can use the experience as a spiritual practice to help you awaken.

Relax as much as you can and come into the present moment. Let go of any thoughts that may be filling your head and focus instead on the feelings you are experiencing in your body. If it is physical suffering, become intensely aware of the physical sensations – the throbbing, stabbing, burning sensations, etc. If it is emotional pain, become aware of exactly how the emotion is manifesting in your body. Is it a gnawing in your guts or the anxious fluttering of anxiety, and so on?

You may find there is strong mental resistance to opening yourself fully to the bodily sensations you are experiencing. If so, try not to get caught in a battle with yourself, but persevere in gently removing your attention from your thoughts and concentrating on your physical sensations.

The more you do this, the more you will discover that these sensations, although perhaps unpleasant and undesirable, are not themselves suffering. Suffering is a name we give to the futile experience of trying to push these experiences away. Let these experiences be, and they will pass when they have run their course, like a spent storm cloud.

66 If you know how to suffer,

you will be able not to suffer.

See through suffering

and you will have nonsuffering. 99

JESUS IN THE ACTS OF JOHN
GNOSTIC GOSPEL

66 Man cannot remake himself without suffering. 99

IRINA TWEEDIE
SUFI TEACHER

Karma

"Karma" in Hindi

THE INDIAN TERM *"Karma" is now familiar in the West. The essence of the doctrine of karma is "Do as you would be done by, for you will be done by as you do!" It predicts that if we treat others well, life will treat us well, but if we treat others badly, life will treat us badly. Here, once again, is the spiritual paradox that if we act selfishly we will suffer, but if we act selflessly we will also benefit.*

COSMIC JUSTICE

Karma is often seen as a system of cosmic justice that explains our present predicament as a reward or punishment for our good and bad actions in the past, both in this life and in previous incarnations. If we accept this idea we will acknowledge that our negative life-situations are of our own making, not the arbitrary result of capricious fate. We will take 100 percent responsibility both for what we do and what is done to us, because they are ultimately the same thing.

ACCUMULATING GOOD KARMA

Seeing karma as a system of cosmic justice that rewards and punishes us is only an analogy, and like all analogies it can be unhelpful as well as illuminating. Spiritual practice can easily become viewed as a way of accumulating "good karma" and so getting an easier ride in life. Actually this sort of self-centered acquisitive attitude only generates more bad karma, because bad karma is always and only a consequence of self-orientation.

KARMA IS OFTEN SEEN AS A SYSTEM OF COSMIC JUSTICE

PAYING OFF BAD KARMA

Seeing our own suffering as an unavoidable process of paying off the debt of "bad karma" can encourage an attitude of passive resignation that prevents us from fully embracing the opportunities life is offering us to grow. The idea of karma as cosmic justice can also become an excuse for not caring for others. It can be a convenient way to dismiss people's misfortunes as retribution for some sinful past life. Actually the spiritual response is to do all in one's power to alleviate their suffering with genuine compassion.

OPPORTUNITY NOT PUNISHMENT

It is more helpful to see the process of karma as offering us opportunities to grow rather than rewarding or punishing us. The Higher Power is better compared to a loving parent whose ways we are not yet mature enough to understand, than some dispassionate, vindictive judge favoring the compliant and condemning the rest to suffer his cosmic vengeance. The process of karma is how life, in its compassion, creates circumstances that show us exactly where we are still caught in the illusion of separateness. Our karma is our curriculum in the school of life. It is not retribution for past crimes, but a chance to discover our essential goodness.

COSMIC KARMA BANK

Dear Sir or Madam,

I regret to inform you that you have run up serious debts of bad karma. Unless you invest some time immediately in accumulating adequate good karma, you will be subject to a series of unpleasant misfortunes until this debt is paid off.

FREE FROM KARMA

Enlightenment is freedom from the effects of karma. However, enlightenment is not the result of finally paying off some sort of cosmic debt. Enlightenment happens when we eventually understand that the whole idea of personal karma accrued by good and bad actions only arises alongside the illusion of being a separate self. An enlightened master is free from personal karma because the master knows he or she is not a person. The master knows there is no such thing as *your karma* or *my karma*. There is only *the karma* – the impersonal process of cause and effect through which the past becomes the future. To be free of karma is to cease believing oneself to be a person being pushed around by events, and instead to be a detached witness to the unfolding of life.

Instant Karma

Our good and bad actions are said to be like seeds, the fruit of which sometimes takes lifetimes to mature. However, the effects of karma are also instantaneous. Acting from our separate self is its own punishment, because we are immediately impoverished by being cut off from our deeper identity. Likewise, acting from the higher Self is its own reward, because we immediately experience our true nature.

Master Pai-chang and the Fox

Master Pai-chang was approached by a fox who told him, "I once was a Zen master like you. One day a student asked me if an enlightened man was subject to the law of karma. I replied, 'The enlightened man rides the wave of karma.' For this error I was condemned to live as a fox. Please help me see my mistake." Master Pai-chang told him, "For the enlightened man, there is only the wave of karma and no one to ride it." His visitor became enlightened and the fox was no more.

ZEN TEACHING STORY

HO'OPONOPONO

Ho'oponopono is an ancient spiritual technique practiced by the shamans of Hawaii, known as "kahunas." The kahunas teach that we create our own reality and that the problems in our lives are the results of "errors" in us. "Ho'oponopono" means "to rectify an error." It is a technique to help us change our lives for the better by taking 100 percent responsibility, not only for our own actions but for all that happens to us and around us.

To practice Ho'oponopono we do not have to analyze our faults endlessly, only take complete responsibility and humbly offer our "errors" up to the Light, which will then transform the situation for the better. Whenever we are confronted with a situation that we find undesirable, we shouldn't blame anyone, but simply apologize to the Light, saying, "I am sorry for whatever it is in me that has brought about this situation," and leave the resolution of the problem to the Power of Life.

HALEAKALA HEW LEN, PH.D.,
HAWAIIAN KAHUNA

" Whatever a man sows,

that he will also reap. "

ST. PAUL

❊❊❊❊

" Whatever affliction may visit you

is what your own hands have earned you. "

KORAN
ISLAMIC SCRIPTURE

❊❊❊❊

" He who understands in truth that he does nothing,

he is not bound by karma. "

THE BHAGAVAD GITA
HINDU SCRIPTURE

" So long as the feeling 'I am doing' is there,

one must experience the result of one's acts,

whether they are good or bad.

If you are not the body

and do not have the idea 'I am the doer,'

the consequences of your good and bad actions

will not affect you. "

RAMANA MAHARISHI
HINDU SAGE

INDIAN ASCETIC

Desire

*I*N THE MODERN WORLD *we have created a new religion of mass consumerism that promises satisfaction by constantly creating and fulfilling an endless succession of desires. Spirituality, however, teaches that this whole endeavor is inevitably doomed to failure. When we get the object of our desire we experience a momentary release from craving. In this transitory experience we glimpse what it is like to be content and at peace with things as they are. But within a short period a new desire has arisen and we are discontent again.*

THE ENDLESS WHEEL

We are caught on an endless wheel of desire, temporary fulfillment, followed by further desire and dissatisfaction. We have finally got the new car we wanted so much and we feel tremendous every time we drive it, but within a few months we have become used to our new possession and crave a bigger better model to give us that feeling of satisfaction. We may be having a perfect vacation that we have looked forward to all year, but as it draws to an end we don't want to go home. We may have at last found the lover of our dreams, but soon we are taking them for granted and want them to be other than they are.

POSSESSIONS BRING TRANSITORY HAPPINESS, NOT LASTING PEACE

DESIRE ADDICTS

Desire is like a drug. We are addicted to more. Whenever we get what we want, it just ups the dose we need to stay even relatively content. Before we got our new car we were relatively content with an old car but desired something better. Now that we have something better, not only do we crave something better still but to go back to the old car would actually make us miserable. Having our desires fulfilled not only fails to make us permanently happy, it actually forces us to maintain a higher level of affluence to just stop us from being unhappy!

DESIRELESSNESS

Spirituality teaches us that it is more awareness, not more possessions, that leads to peace. Satisfaction is lack of desire, yet our endless desires can never fully and finally be satisfied. So, the saints and sages urge us to cultivate a state of desirelessness; to surrender our personal cravings

and accept "what is." Desirelessness is not cold indifference. It is wanting everything as much as everything else. It is a fundamental YES to whatever life is offering. It is saying to the Higher Power "I want what you give me."

ONE ALL-CONSUMING DESIRE

The saints and sages teach us to concentrate all of our desires into the one all-consuming desire for communion with God. Yet to truly transcend our separate self, we must even abandon the desire for God or enlightenment or whatever name we give to the spiritual goal. Hindus use the metaphor of a priest stoking a funeral pyre with a stick to make sure the corpse is completely turned to ash, before finally also throwing the stick into the flames. The corpse represents the illusion of the separate self that is consumed in the flames of spiritual illumination, and the stick is the desire for God that is the last desire to be abandoned. The Christian mystic Meister Eckhart calls this final state of utter desirelessness "spiritual poverty." He writes:

"We must become truly poor and as free from our own will as when we were born. I tell you, by the eternal truth, so long as you even desire to fulfill the will of God and hanker after eternity, you are not truly poor. Only someone who wills nothing, knows nothing, and desires nothing, has true spiritual poverty."

THE FUEL OF LIFE

Yet desire is the impulse that pushes us onward. It is the fuel of life. We would not eat if it were not for hunger. We would not drink if it were not for thirst. The saints and sages aren't recommending being inert and unmotivated. They are urging us to see desire for want it is – an inner restlessness that promises satisfaction but actually just disrupts our natural state of peace and equilibrium. Spirituality is not about having no desires, it is about not being controlled by our appetites. It is about being free to act consciously in a wholesome way, not being unconsciously driven by the personal cravings of the separate self.

HINDU PRIESTS IN A RELIGIOUS PROCESSION

HINDU FUNERAL PYRE

EXPLORING DESIRE

Whenever you feel compelled by desire, don't just get unconsciously swept along by your habitual addiction to more. Set yourself free. Go inside and confront the compulsion with the knowledge that desirelessness, not constant desire, is the route to peace and contentment.

- Focus on the desire and notice what feelings and thoughts accompany it.
- Does it make you agitated and anxious?
- Does it distract your attention from the miracle of the here and now?
- Ask yourself why you desire what you desire.
- What is it you hope to feel by having the desire fulfilled?
- Is it the fulfillment of your desire that you crave or the feeling of satisfaction that accompanies the absence of desire?

What does fulfillment mean to you?

66 The individual 'I' exists for as long as there is desire for pleasure. No worldly delight is comparable to the delight that will fill your heart when you completely abandon all hopes and desires. 99

MAHARAMAYANA
HINDU SCRIPTURE

❦❦❦❦

66 All your suffering comes from desiring things that cannot be had. Stop desiring and you won't suffer. 99

JALAL AL-DIN RUMI
SUFI SAGE

❦❦❦❦

66 I have only one desire,
to disappear into God,
to be submerged in his peace. 99

THOMAS MERTON
CHRISTIAN MYSTIC

❦❦❦❦

66 To take pleasure in everything,
desire to take pleasure in nothing.
To possess everything,
desire to possess nothing.
To be everything,
desire to be nothing.
To know everything,
desire to know nothing. 99

ST. JOHN OF THE CROSS
CHRISTIAN MYSTIC

THE PROCESSION, BY PRJANISCHNIKOW

Nonattachment

A STUDENT ONCE HAD *a private audience with a renowned Buddhist master. Entering the master's small room, the student was struck by a beautiful golden Buddha and casually remarked, "What a beautiful statue." "Do you think so?" replied the master. "Then please let me give it to you." In this gesture of generosity the master was giving the student something far more precious than any precious ornament. He was teaching by example the important spiritual quality of nonattachment.*

SIDDHARTA

THE ORIGIN OF SUFFERING

The saints and sages teach us to be unattached to the transitory things of life, such as wealth, success, and even our own body and our loved ones. By their very nature all such things must eventually pass away. If we are free from attachments, we will accept the comings and goings of life with equanimity. If not, we will suffer. This is why the Buddha taught, "The origin of all suffering is selfish desire and attachment."

LOVE IS NONATTACHMENT

It may sound cold and inhuman not to be attached to the people we love, but being unattached is not the same as being indifferent or unloving. Actually it is the complete opposite. Attachments trap us in our separate self. Only when we are free of attachments are we liberated from our personal self-interest and able to fully express the deep compassion of our true nature. Nonattachment is not unfeeling. It is loving without expecting anything in return. It is letting things come, fully appreciating them in the moment, and then letting them go. It is not grasping after shadows. It is not trying to force the flow of life to follow the particular direction that fits our personal desires.

WE ARE ALREADY UNATTACHED

It is not that we should be nonattached and that failing to be so is some sort of moral sin. It is rather that if we see things as they really are, we will perceive that we are not actually attached to anything, but only temporarily seem to be. If enough time passes, we find that people, situations, and things to which we once felt extremely attached no longer have such a powerful hold over us. The spiritual masters are asking us to recognize now that our attachments are only passing illusions. In reality we are always unattached.

BECOME A PASSERBY

Islamic scripture recommends, "Be in the world as if you were a stranger or a traveler." In the Gnostic Gospel of Thomas, Jesus, likewise, advises, "Become a passer-by." We are only temporary visitors to an impermanent world, and by cultivating detachment we relinquish the impossible struggle to find permanence anywhere but within Consciousness itself.

WHETHER WE LIKE IT OR NOT THE PAST HAS GONE

Zen Master Dogen

Zen master Dogen taught that religious rituals are completely unnecessary to achieve enlightenment. All that was required was to cultivate complete nonattachment. He writes:

"Burning incense, bowing before the Buddha, offering prayers, confessing your sins, and reading the scriptures – from the very start of one's spiritual practice these are all completely unnecessary. Liberate yourself from your attachments to body and mind – this is the only requirement. Become the Buddha. If you do, your ecstatic meditations will transform the whole universe into enlightenment."

ZEN MASTER DOGEN

66 One should use one's mind in such a way that it is free from any attachment. 99

THE DIAMOND SUTRA
BUDDHIST SCRIPTURE

66 The greatest generosity is nonattachment. 99

ATISHA
BUDDHIST SAGE

Robbing Ramana Maharshi's Ashram

When a group of thieves broke into Ramana Maharshi's ashram, the renown Hindu sage apologized that there was so little for them to steal and told his devotees to let the thieves take whatever they wished. He explained, "The thieves have their nature and we have ours. It is for us to bear and forbear, so we should not interfere with them."

The Thief and the Monk

A thief went to rob an isolated hermitage, but found only an old monk meditating in his empty cell. Seeing the thief's disappointment, the monk offered him his only possession – the blanket he was wrapped in. As the confused thief left, the monk looked out of the open window at the beautiful full moon and mused to himself sadly, "If only I could have given him this glorious moon."

ZEN TEACHING STORY

Master Mu-nan's Nonattachment

Zen master Mu-nan was renowned for his non-attachment. But, although he had indeed let go of all worldly things, he was still attached to the teachings and traditions of Zen. This last attachment was shown to him by his pupil Shoju. When Mu-nan came to make Shoju his successor, he reverentially handed him an old book, saying, "This book of wisdom has been written in by generations of masters. I myself have added my own comments and understanding. Now it is yours."

Shoju was disinterested. "I learned Zen from you without words," he said. "I have no use for this book – you keep it."

"It belongs to you as a symbol of the teachings you have received. Here, it is yours," insisted Mu-nan. Shoju took the book and casually threw it into the fire they were both warming themselves around. Mu-nan, who never got angry, jumped up yelling, "What are you doing?"

Shoju responded calmly, "What are you saying?"

ZEN TEACHING STORY

66 He who bends to himself a joy
Does the wing'd life destroy;
But he who kisses the joy as it flies
Lives in eternity's sunrise. 99

WILLIAM BLAKE
MYSTICAL POET

❦❦❦❦

66 Those overtaken by a storm when traveling by sea don't worry about their luggage, but throw it overboard with their own hands, considering their property to be less important than their lives. So why don't we, following this example, throw out whatever drags our soul down to the depths. 99

ST. NELIOS THE ASCETIC
CHRISTIAN SAGE

TIBETAN MANDALA

THE GIVE AWAY

The Native Americans have a beautiful ceremony, called the "Give Away," that teaches nonattachment. This is an inspiring ritual you can perform with a group of spiritual friends. All participants sit in a sacred circle and each places in the center an object that is precious to that person as an offering. Each participant takes a new object from the circle and relinquishes his or her own valued possession to another.

You can also explore the power of giving away what you value by selecting something that you find particularly precious and giving it to someone who you feel would appreciate it. You could give it to a friend, but it is even more powerful if it is a complete stranger whom you will never see again and from whom you can expect nothing back in return. Either way you will find that you have gained far more than you have lost.

Fear

FEAR IS A STULTIFYING emotion. It prevents us from plunging into life, keeping us hovering on the sidelines anxious for our safety. Day in and day out most of us are full of little worries and anxieties that poison our appreciation of the miracle of existence. And these are only a thin veneer covering deeper more disturbing fears, too terrifying even to contemplate: the fear of death, of loss, of suffering, of meaninglessness.

A SHAMAN DESCENDS TO THE UNDERWORLD

A NEGATIVE FORM OF DESIRE

Fear is a negative form of desire. It is a desire for things not to be a certain way in the future. Both fear and desire are rooted in the past. Desire is the memory of pleasure that we seek to repeat, and fear is the memory of pain that we seek to avoid. Fear and desire are our projections of the past into the future, which prevent us from fully experiencing the present.

FACING FEAR TAKES COURAGE

THE LOGIC OF FEAR

Although fear and worry seem to be completely unhelpful experiences in every way, the truth is that if we identify exclusively with our separate self, fear is unavoidable. It is a logical reaction to the facts, for it is all too clear that life has little reverence for us as individual beings. It has no compunction in exploding a volcano and devouring whole cities. It has no hesitation in unleashing some horrific epidemic on young and old alike. Everything it creates, including ourselves, it unsentimentally destroys. It is a dangerous world for a separate self and, if we believe that this is our ultimate identity, we should be afraid – very afraid.

A PRODUCT OF SEPARATENESS

Spirituality, however, teaches that this is not our true identity. Fear is a byproduct of believing ourselves to be a separate self. It is also, therefore, a signpost that shows us where we are still clinging to this illusion. When we turn and face our fear, we turn and face out spiritual ignorance. If we know that our essential nature is beyond birth and death, we can, with confidence, undergo the process of life that will reveal this nature to us. We can trust that we are in the divine care of the Higher Power and need not be anxious. As it says in the Muslim Koran "Someone who believes in his Lord has no fear."

Fear of Failure

Fear of failure holds many people back from fully entering into life. It can prevent us from having the courage to commit to the journey of awakening, because we have already decided that we could never be enlightened – that's for other "special" people. If we never try, at least we will never fail. But what is failure and why should we fear it?

The Freedom to Fail

Everyone knows the pain, frustration, and disappointment of failure. Everyone has broken dreams – divorce, bankruptcy, a bad habit that just won't go, trust that is betrayed, artistic projects not appreciated, scientific theories proven wrong. We invest a lot of our time and emotion in something and then things don't turn out the way we expected. For every person who succeeds, there are, inevitably, many more who fail. Only one person can win the race. Not everyone can be rich and famous. There are many books that deal with "how to succeed," some of which contain valuable insights. But the value and importance of failure is usually ignored. Spirituality wants us to be free to succeed, but it also wants us to be free to fail. It just wants us to be free.

Disillusioned

Spirituality sees failure as an inevitable and natural part of the journey of awakening, not as a purely negative experience. Failure often leaves us feeling profoundly disillusioned. But is it necessarily a bad thing to be "dis-illusioned"? Do we want "illusion" in our lives? Failure exposes just how wrapped up in illusion we are. It forces us to acknowledge that we are not in control of our lives after all. It confronts us with our attachments. It reminds us that life is not about "winning," it is about awakening. It helps us take ourselves less seriously.

FEAR OF FAILURE CAN LEAD TO STRESS AND DEPRESSION

Fail Better

Broken dreams may break the emotional heart, but when the emotional heart is broken open, it is an opportunity to discover the spiritual heart inside. Broken dreams are a part of the process of healing the sickness of separateness. There is no failure on the spiritual path, because each disappointment is a precious opportunity to grow as a person or even to transcend the personality altogether and become the detached witness of our changing fortunes. It is a chance to succeed in "letting go and letting God." When we understand this we can unreservedly enter the turmoil of life. As the playwright Samuel Beckett puts it, we can simply say "No matter. Try again. Fail again. Fail better."

TRANSFORMING FEAR

Fear is not just a negative experience. It can be a great spiritual teacher. It reveals how attached we are to the separate self. It presents us with the opportunity to develop courage. It puts our spirituality to the test and shows how deep or superficial our understanding really is. Many spiritual practices deliberately seek out ways to confront us with our fears, so that through the experience fear can be conquered. In many shamanic cultures, for example, young men and women go through terrifying initiations to put them in direct contact with the spirit and bring them into full adulthood. Through fearlessly facing fear, fear is overcome.

1 *Focus in on a particular fear. Instead of pushing it away as an enemy, welcome it in as a great teacher. Ask it to aid you on your spiritual path.*

2 *Pay close attention to how it makes you feel and the anxious thoughts it provokes. See if it is showing you where you are still identified with your separate self.*

3 *Explore the opportunities it is presenting to you to develop the quality of courage.*

The Trials of The Hero

In Greek myth, Heracles, known to the Romans as Hercules, was set twelve trials by the goddess Hera. These twelve tasks, which corresponded to the twelve signs of the zodiac, not only required the hero to display great courage, they also required great wisdom, including the ability to develop his "feminine side" by dressing as a woman. In the Pagan Mystery religion, these trials were understood as allegories for the challenges an initiate on the spiritual path must face to overcome fear and ignorance.

A STATUE OF HERCULES

❝ Who can add anything to his life through being anxious? ❞

JESUS
GOSPEL OF MATTHEW

❧❧❧❧

❝ You are Father, Mother, Friend, Brother, With You as succorer in all places, what fear have I? ❞

GURU NANAK
SIKH SAINT

❧❧❧❧

❝ There is no fear in love, for perfect love casts out fear. ❞

ST. JOHN
NEW TESTAMENT

❧❧❧❧

❝ 'I am not, nor will I be. I have nothing, nor will I have.' This frightens the immature but dispels all fear in the wise. ❞

NAGARJUNA
BUDDHIST SAINT

ST. MATTHEW

Impermanence

EVERYTHING THAT COMES into being soon starts to decay and pass away. In many traditions this is taken as a sign that the world is an illusion. Reality, it is argued, must be permanent and eternal, not fleeting and ephemeral. The impermanent world of the senses is only relatively real. It is a sort of dream, an illusionary play of transitory forms, which the Hindus call "maya" and the Buddhists call "samsara."

APPEARANCES IN CONSCIOUSNESS

What we perceive as an objective reality is actually made up of appearances in Consciousness. The underlying reality is not the world, but the Consciousness that perceives it. We experience Consciousness as our permanent but ineffable sense of "I am." This is the still point at our very center that silently witnesses the fluctuating flurry of sensations that we call the world.

SEEK THE PERMANENT REALITY OF CONSCIOUSNESS

The spiritual masters encourage us to invest less energy trying to accumulate such things as wealth, social status, and material security, for these are only valuable in terms of a world that is at best only relatively real and will inevitably pass away. We should rather, as Jesus teaches, "lay up our treasure where rust and moths cannot corrupt it" and discover the underlying permanent reality of the Self. Only the witnessing Consciousness we think of as our "I" is always present. It is like an empty space within which things appear and decay. The space alone is eternal and everlasting.

ALL FORMS OF LIFE ARE TRANSIENT

BEING THE WITNESS

An interesting way to cultivate a detached awareness of the world as an illusionary play of appearances is to watch a movie at the cinema, but, as a spiritual practice, try to remain conscious that you are watching an illusion.

Don't get sucked into the story and forget that you are actually sitting there in the dark and will go home afterward. This is not the best way to appreciate a good movie, but it will help you develop the witnessing consciousness.

When you leave the movie theater, experiment with watching life as if it were a movie, in which you yourself are one of the characters, coming and going as the script demands.

Security or Sarcophagus?
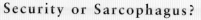

There once was a king who was so frightened that a great calamity would soon befall him that he built a room of solid rock to hide within and surrounded it by guards. When he was in it, he noticed a little chink of light, which he filled in to prevent any harm from reaching him. Thus he became a prisoner and died in that room. In his hopeless search for security in this impermanent world he tried to build a safe haven, but ended up creating a coffin.

SUFI TEACHING STORY

66 Phenomena are real when experienced as the Self, and illusory when seen apart from the Self. 99

RAMANA MAHARSHI
HINDU SAGE

❀❀❀❀

66 You will never be satisfied with impermanent, passing things, for you were not created to find your rest in them. 99

THOMAS À KEMPIS
CHRISTIAN SAGE

BIRTH OF KRISHNA

Death and reincarnation

THE ONLY CERTAIN THING *about our life is that it will end in death. Yet all spiritual traditions are agreed that death is but a new beginning. They suggest that death is not the perpetual darkness that some fear, but on the contrary is an experience of overwhelming light. Some spiritual traditions, such as Tibetan Buddhism, have amassed huge amounts of information about dying and the after-life states. The Tibetan Book of the Dead is a scripture which is read out loud to dying people to help them use the process of death as an opportunity to attain enlightenment. It describes death as an encounter with a Being of Light which it identifies as our own true nature – pure Consciousness itself.*

THE CYCLE OF REINCARNATION

THE EARTHLY
PARADISE AND THE
ASCENT TO THE
HEAVENLY PARADISE,
PAINTED BY
HIERONYMUS BOSCH

NEAR-DEATH EXPERIENCES

Many thousands of reports have been amassed of ordinary people who describe extraordinary spiritual experiences when facing death. Research has shown that most terminally ill patients who are conscious at the time of death experience vivid visions of "indescribable beauty." Those pulled back from the brink of death by modern medicine return with wondrous tales of having left their body and encountered a Being of Light and Love, of meeting their dead friends and relatives, and understanding from a detached and impartial viewpoint the consequences of the choices they had made in life. Most find such experiences utterly transform their lives in a spiritual, but not necessarily religious, way. The modern mystic and psychologist Carl Jung wrote of his own near-death experience:

> "What happens after death is so unspeakably glorious that our imagination and feelings do not suffice to form even an approximate conception of it."

REINCARNATION

The majority of spiritual traditions teach that after death we reincarnate into another human body to continue our journey of spiritual evolution. Between death and rebirth we experience various heavenly or hellish states, as a reward or punishment for the way we have lived our earthly life. This is taught by Hinduism, Buddhism, Taoism, and Shamanic traditions, as well as by mystics within other traditions such as the Jewish Cabalists, the Gnostic Christians, and the Islamic Sufis.

NO BIRTH, NO DEATH

From the enlightened perspective, reincarnation is only relatively real. The soul that travels through many births and deaths may be a higher form of our identity than the mortal body and personality, but is not our true nature – the ineffable "I" of pure Consciousness. As the mystic scholar Dr. W. Y. Evans-Wentz writes: "The knower itself neither incarnates nor reincarnates – it is the Spectator." The enlightened masters teach that ultimately there is no separate identity that incarnates in the first place. We are undying because we are unborn. It is only the illusion of a separate self that experiences the cycle of rebirth. Death is an opportunity to awaken from this illusion and know our true nature as the eternal witness of both life and death. The great Hindu sage Ramana Maharshi explains:

"If a man considers that he is born, he cannot avoid the fear of death. Let him find out if he has been born or if the Self has any birth. He will discover that the Self always exists, that the body which is born resolves itself into thought and that the emergence of thought is the root of all mischief. Find from where thoughts emerge. Then you will be able to abide in the ever-present inmost Self and be free from the idea of birth or the fear of death."

The Ultimate Mystery

Many sages teach that death is meant to be the ultimate mystery and we should focus on the here and now life rather than speculating about the after-life. When Zen master Gudo was asked "What happens to an enlightened man after death?" he replied "How should I know, I haven't died yet."

66 Death is not the extinguishing of the light, but the blowing out of the candle because the dawn has come. 99

RABINDRANATH TAGORE
HINDU SAGE

❧❧❧❧

66 Human beings can't begin to conceive what awaits them at death. 99

HERACLITUS
PAGAN SAGE

❧❧❧❧

66 To die is different from What anyone supposes And luckier. 99

WALT WHITMAN
MYSTICAL POET

WALT WHITMAN

TOMORROW MAY BE TOO LATE

For many people death is a disturbing prospect, not only because it is the great unknown but because there may be much in their lives left unresolved: things that need to be said, wounds that need to be healed, loved ones left unappreciated, and so on. Most of us put up with years of partial communication until it is too late. This exercise uses the awareness of death to give you the motivation to break through the barriers of fear and inertia that prevent you from opening your heart.

1 *Sit quietly and imagine yourself unexpectedly on your deathbed surrounded by your loved ones.*

2 *What is it you need to tell them? Have you taken the time lately to let them know how much you love and value them? What enmities and resentments need healing?*

3 *Whatever it is you need to do or say resolve to do or say it today. Don't hesitate. Tomorrow may be too late. Let the awareness of death give you the motivation to break through the barriers of fear and inertia that prevent you from opening your heart.*

OPEN YOUR HEART

Be here now

HERE AND NOW is the only reality. The past is a story we tell based on hazy recollections. The future is a daydream produced by our hopes and fears. No matter how difficult the present may seem to us, it is inevitably richer than any fantasy of the future or memory of the past. These are only virtual realities. They have no substance. Here and now is always preferable, because only here and now IS. This is where life is really happening.

ONLY THIS MOMENT IS REAL

THE IMMEDIACY OF THE MOMENT

We are always here and now, but our attention is often lost in regrets about the past and anxieties about the future. Spirituality teaches us to concentrate our attention in the immediacy of the moment, to be fully present in what we are doing, to approach each instant as a new and rich experience, not be lost in our thoughts about life but to really hear, see, and feel. The Zen masters, in particular, emphasize the need to find the quality they call "beginner's mind" in which we are always fresh and uncluttered by our preconceptions based on the past. When Zen master T'sui-wei was asked "What is Buddhism?" he simply whispered, "Look how splendid these bamboos are!" Zen Master Huang-po teaches, "Here it is – right now. Start thinking about it and you miss it."

DOORWAY TO ETERNITY

Spirituality teaches us to focus on the here and now, yet ironically the more we do the more it becomes apparent that in this world of constant flux there is no definable "moment," only the unceasing flow of the Tao. When we search for the now we do not find it. Instead we discover perpetual change. To experience this fully is to have one's being outside time, witnessing the coming and going of thoughts and sensations that we call time. In searching for the here and now we discover a doorway to eternity.

APPRECIATE THE BEAUTY OF THE HERE AND NOW

BEING PRESENT

Bringing your awareness into the present moment is a spiritual technique you can practice anywhere at anytime. Do it right now – this instant.

1 *Be alive to the magic of the moment. Become fully conscious of the flow of sensual experience. Really see, hear, taste, and touch all that is around you.*

2 *We often find it refreshing to be around small children because they appreciate the ordinary miracles of life that we take for granted. Allow yourself to experience life once again with the freshness of a child.*

3 *When you feel you have lost your awareness of the moment just say to yourself "Now!"*

Here and now is where you are so it is obviously where life wants you to be – what gifts is the moment offering you that you are overlooking?

66 His disciples said to him 'When will the kingdom come?' Jesus said, 'It will not come by waiting for it. The kingdom of the Father is spread out upon the earth, and men do not see it.' 99

JESUS
GNOSTIC GOSPEL
OF THOMAS

66 How can I know anything about the past or the future, when the light of the Beloved shines only NOW. 99

JALAL AL-DIN RUMI
SUFI SAGE

*RECOVER THE SPONTANEITY
OF CHILDHOOD*

Taking things lightly

LIFE CAN OFTEN *seem to be a serious business. This can turn it into a solemn drudge or, worse still, a painful ordeal, or perhaps worst of all something from which we escape into numb indifference. Spirituality teaches us to lighten up and see the humor of our predicament. The first time many people see through the illusion of all they have taken life to be, they experience an ecstatic release of tension that expresses itself in uncontrollable laughter. The delightfully irreverent modern American spiritual teacher Ram Dass calls this the "Cosmic Giggle." It is the belly laugh of God delighting in the wonderful absurdity of creation.*

IT'S GOOD TO LAUGH

CRAZY WISDOM

Many of the great spiritual masters have become renowned for their crazy ways. For example, Ram Dass' Hindu guru Neem Karoli Baba would sometimes be found contentedly sitting in a pile of manure on the road. Zen master Chao-chou once responded to a question by removing his straw sandals, putting them on his head, and leaving the room. Such bizarre actions shock us out of our habitual "serious" states of mind into the freshness of the spontaneous NOW. They set us free from the confines of normality and open the door to dancing with delight, rejoicing at the preposterously implausible nature of life.

PLAYING AT LIFE

The Hindus call life God's "lila" or game. How can we play at life as if it were a game? A game has goals that we strive to reach, which give it purpose and make it exciting. However, if we forget it's only a game, then winning and losing can start to become far more important than they actually are. The real purpose of playing a game is to enjoy the playing. Spirituality helps to prevent us from getting bogged down in being too serious, and allows us to enjoy the game of life.

PLAYING OUR PART

Life is sometimes compared to a cosmic drama in which God is the playwright and director and we are the characters walking on the stage of the world. The Power of Life has laid on a tremendous show for us – what a waste this would all be if we didn't enjoy it.

> " Remember the whole thing is just a play and the Lord has assigned you a part. Act your part well; there all your duty ends. He has designed the play and he enjoys it. "
>
> SAI BABA
> HINDU GURU

"Human beings are puppets of God and this is the best thing about them. We should all play our parts as perfectly as possible."

PLATO
PAGAN SAGE

"He who faultlessly acts the drama of life that God has given him to play, knows what is to be done and what is to be endured."

CLEMENT OF ALEXANDRIA
CHRISTIAN MYSTIC

Heavenly Clowns

Rabbi Baruqa of Huza often went to the marketplace at Lapet. One day, the prophet Elijah appeared to him there, and Rabbi Baruqa asked him, "Is there anyone among all these people who will have a share in the World to Come?" Elijah answered, "There is none." Later, two men came to the marketplace, and Elijah said to Rabbi Baruqa, "Those two will have a share in the World to Come!" Rabbi Baruqa asked the newcomers, "What is your occupation?" They replied, "We are clowns. When we see someone who is sad, we cheer them up. When we see two people quarreling, we try to make peace between them."

JEWISH TEACHING STORY

Breaking the Rules

Two Buddhist monks who had taken a solemn vow never even to look at a woman were walking home toward their monastery when they came to a fast-flowing river. On the banks of the river they found a young girl frightened to try to cross the raging torrent. One of the monks, who was a youthful novice, dutifully turned his eyes away and began to cross the water. The other monk, who was his elderly teacher, walked over to the girl, lifted her upon his shoulders, and carried her across to the other side. Several hours after this incident, as the monks continued their silent journey home, the young novice could contain himself no longer and exclaimed, "I don't understand master. We have taken a solemn vow not even to look at a woman, let alone pick one up and carry her. How could you betray our holy orders?" "What?" replied the old master smiling, "are you still carrying that young woman? I put her down on the bank of the river."

BUDDHIST TEACHING STORY

BE YOUR OWN ZEN MASTER!

Do you need to lighten up? Then be your own Zen master and break out of the prison of being overserious.

Think of a bizarre action you could perform – something completely out of character. It could be shouting a meaningless word, or hopping on one leg, or taking off a shoe and putting it on your head like master Chao-chou: the more absurd the better.

Whenever you find yourself taking yourself too seriously be your own Zen master by performing your bizarre act. It will feel very strange, but that's the whole point. You'll find you can't take yourself so seriously when you're behaving in a strange, uncharacteristic way. Every time you do this it will become easier and easier to lighten up and see the humour of your predicament and the absurdity of making it into a "big deal."

BREAK OUT FROM THE ORDINARY AND LIGHTEN UP

❝ Angels can fly because they take

themselves so lightly. ❞

NEW AGE SAYING

✢✢✢✢

❝ I am your playmate.
I will lead the child within you
on a wonderful adventure
that I have chosen for you. ❞

GOD
SPEAKING TO CHRISTIAN MYSTIC
MECHTILD OF MAGDEBURG

❝ The world exists only as an appearance.
From beginning to end it is a playful game. ❞

SHABISTARI
SUFI SAGE

✢✢✢✢

❝ How remarkable!
In Me the limitless ocean,
the waves of individual selves
arise according to their inherent nature,
meet and play with one another for a while
and then disappear. ❞

ASHTAVAKRA GITA
HINDU SCRIPTURE

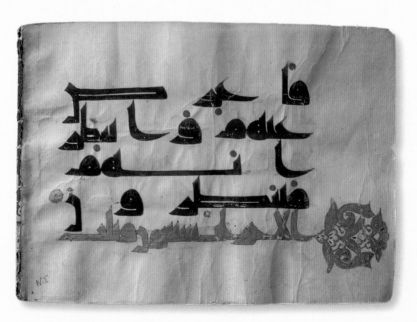

ISLAMIC INSCRIPTIONS FROM THE KORAN

Freedom and fate

MANY SPIRITUAL TRADITIONS *teach that, although we think we are in charge of our lives, in reality we are not. Free will is an illusion created alongside the illusion of being a separate individual. To the ego, such fatalism seems like the ultimate effrontery. Human dignity seems to require us to acknowledge that we are fundamentally free. But what does our so-called freedom really mean? We do not choose to be born or when we will die. We do not choose our bodies or personal idiosyncrasies. We do not choose our families or our environment.*

THE WHEEL OF FATE

THERE IS NO WAY OF KNOWING WHERE OUR LIVES WILL LEAD US

WHAT FREEDOM?

Most of what makes us who we are is clearly beyond our control. But what of our personal decisions? We reach a fork in the road and, although we have no control over what awaits us on the road we end up traveling, it does seem as if we can choose to go left or right. But what informs this so-called choice? We do not choose the information that is available to help us evaluate the situation. We do not even choose what thoughts we think when we deliberate upon our decision – they spontaneously arise into consciousness from who knows where. Even if we do have the choice to turn left or right, is this choice meaningful? We will never be able to compare the results of our decision with what would have happened if we had chosen differently – this is impossible for us ever to discover. So we can never truly say that any decision was either good or bad, because there is no way of knowing. Personal free will, it would seem, is not all it is cracked up to be!

A PHILOSOPHY OF SERVITUDE?

The mystics teach that there are no single events – such as individual choices. Every event is actually an aspect of the one event – the metamorphosing Oneness of Reality. Free will is a subjective illusion. Life is the unfolding of fate. There is no "you" or "I" to make a choice. Everything happens through God's grace. This can seem like a philosophy of servitude. But the mystics are not teaching that our "selves" are being controlled by some manipulating "outside" entity. It is rather that everything is a manifestation of One Self – our true identity of which most of us are ignorant.

SURRENDER

The mystics teach that free will is only a corollary of the illusion of being a person. They urge us to abandon our sense of personal "doership" and surrender to God (while adding, of course, that whether we do or not is beyond our control since we have no control!). Surrender is generally understood as giving up the futile endeavor of trying to control life and instead "letting go and letting God." Because we were never the "doer" in the first place, surrender is merely relinquishing what we never had.

FREEDOM THROUGH SUBMISSION

Ironically, it is through submission that we find spiritual freedom. Without the concept of free will there is freedom from blaming others or feelings of guilt, for there is no one to judge. There is freedom from arrogance and pride, for we have done nothing to be worthy of it. There is freedom from anxiety, for we have no opportunity to affect our fate. There is freedom from ambition, for we have no way of achieving anything. There is freedom from dissatisfaction, because everything is known to be the will of the Higher Power. There is freedom, in short, from all the burdens that identification with the ego lays on our shoulders. No wonder the saints and sages describe the experience of surrender as a blissful experience of release.

Letting Go and Letting God

For many on the spiritual path, surrender comes when we are finally exhausted with trying to bend life to our desires. Bloody, waving a white flag, and crawling on our knees, we come before the Higher Power and confess, "I'm making a mess of things, please take over." But we do not have to wait until life, in its compassion and generosity, forces a reluctant surrender upon us. While we have the subjective experience of free will, we can choose to make one final choice and surrender control of our lives. This may be the only meaningful choice we will ever make.

An age-old technique for doing this is to live with the maxim "Not as I will it, but as You will it." This requires us to let go of how we think it should be and just let things be. The Taoists call this "going with the Tao." But this does not require us to be like dead fish being born along by the current. We do not have to be forever inactive. In fact this is impossible, for life forces action upon us at every moment. Even subjectively choosing to do nothing is experienced as an act of personal will, not surrender. We do not have to stop "doing," only to surrender the idea that we are the "doer." This, the great sages teach, is enlightenment.

> 66 God demands nothing less than complete self-surrender as the price of the only real freedom worth having. 99

MAHATMA GANDHI
INDIAN SPIRITUAL LEADER

⁂

> 66 Sanctity consists in willing what happens to us by God's order. 99

J. P. DE CAUSSADE
CHRISTIAN MYSTIC

⁂

> 66 Those whose spiritual awareness has been awakened never make a false move.
> They don't have to avoid evil.
> They are so replete with love that whatever they do is a good action.
> They are fully conscious that they are not the doer of their actions, but only servants of God. 99

RAMAKRISHNA
HINDU SAGE

Enlightenment

*T*HE GREAT GOAL *of the spiritual path is enlightenment. Yet from the mystical perspective there is no such thing as an enlightened person. Enlightenment is the impersonal realization that everything is One and that the separate person we believe ourselves to be is actually just another passing phenomenon being witnessed by Consciousness. What we take to be our thoughts, feelings, and actions are seen to be just happening as naturally as the sun sets and the rain falls.*

LOTUS FLOWERS

ENLIGHTENMENT IS NATURAL

Spirituality is about expanding the bubble of our personal consciousness. Enlightenment is what happens when the bubble bursts and we merge with impersonal Consciousness. When this occurs we discover that being enlightened is our natural state, unclouded by the illusion of separateness. The great mystics have an ironic sense of humor because they see the absurdity of our predicament. We are seeking so earnestly to become what we already are!

NO WAY TO ENLIGHTENMENT

Enlightenment is not something that can be achieved. Indeed it is the realization that there is no one to achieve anything. Enlightenment is not something that we can strive for. If we believe we are doing anything in order to become enlightened, we are just entrapping ourselves further in the illusion of being a doer. Enlightenment is the understanding that there is no doer. Enlightenment either happens or it doesn't. It's no good worrying about it and useless to strive for it. We are in a natural process of spiritual maturation and the best thing we can do is just let it organically unfold.

LETTING ENLIGHTENMENT HAPPEN

Lying on a bed trying desperately to sleep only gets in the way of sleep naturally occurring when we are tired enough. In the same way struggling to become enlightenment just hampers the process of enlightenment naturally and spontaneously occurring. The best way to fall asleep is to prepare a comfortable bed and relax. Similarly, the sages advise us to prepare ourselves through spiritual practice but to let go of worrying about the results. Yet for enlightenment to occur we must completely understand that everything, including our spiritual practice, is a product of the impersonal life-process.

> 66 The understanding of Truth cannot be achieved.
> It can only happen.
> And when it comes, it cannot be accepted
> unless the mind is empty of 'me'
> and the heart is full of love. 99
>
> RAMESH BALSEKAR
> HINDU SAGE

> 66 Years of digging the earth searching for the blue sky,
> piling up layer upon layer of mediocrity.
> Then one dark night the ceiling blew off,
> and the whole structure disappeared into emptiness. 99
>
> MUSO
> ZEN POET

NO ONE DOES ANYTHING!

If we are the "thinker" of our thoughts, then surely we should be able to stop thinking? This exercise is about attempting to stop thinking and discovering that thoughts keep coming whether we will them or not.

They have a life of their own. They emerge into our consciousness from who knows where, whether we like it or not.

To acknowledge this is a powerfully transformative spiritual experience, for if our thoughts are wholly beyond our control, it no longer makes sense to say that we are doing the thinking. Thoughts are passing phenomena witnessed by Consciousness.

Because all actions issue from thoughts, it makes no sense to see ourselves as the doer of anything. Everything is One, and the decisions and actions that we habitually claim as ours are just another expression of this Oneness.

1 *Sit quietly with your eyes closed and become aware of your thoughts coming and going.*

2 *Now fix firmly in your mind the intention to stop the flow of thoughts.*

3 *Every time you find yourself thinking, just suppress the thought with the counter-thought "Don't think!"*

4 *Remember to watch out for sly little thoughts such as "Wow! I'm sure I stopped thinking then!"*

After you have practiced this exercise for a while, stop trying to suppress your thoughts and become passively aware of their coming and going. You are not the "thinker," you are the witnessing Consciousness.

Mystical union

ENLIGHTENMENT IS THE *dissolution of the separate self into the sublime Oneness. Taoists talk of merging with Tao. Buddhists describe entering state of Nirvana in which the self dissolves into the ocean of Being. The Islamic Sufis experience "Fana fi Allah," the extinguishing of the ego into Allah. Christians enjoy mystical communion with God, which is the true "I." Hindus discover that "Atman is Brahman" – "the true Self is God." We need not fear this dis-appearance into the Ground of Being. This is our true nature. Nothing is lost except the appearance of being a separate self.*

ZEN

WE ARE GOD LOOKING FOR HIMSELF

The Sufi sage Ibn Arabi teaches that God created human beings so that through them He could come to know Himself and that when the seeker finds God, God is recognizing Himself. For the Oneness to be conscious of itself, it becomes two – experiencer and experienced, self and other. We are that Oneness become two. The spiritual path is the process through which we remember ourselves as the One.

"I AM GOD!"

The experience of enlightenment has led many great masters to declare boldly "I am God." This can sound grandiose and self-important, but if the separate self has been genuinely abandoned it is not. As the great Sufi sage Jalal al-Din Rumi explains:

"Don't think that saying 'I am God' is proclaiming one's greatness. It is actually total humility. Someone who says 'I am the servant of God' infers two – God and himself – whereas someone who says 'I am God' negates himself. He relinquishes his own existence. 'I am God' means 'I don't exist. Everything is God. Only God exists. I am nothing. I am utter emptiness.' This is complete humility, not arrogance, but people often misunderstand. When

someone says he is God's servant, he still sees himself as a doer, albeit in God's service. He is not yet drowned in the ocean of God. When he is, there will be no such thing as 'his actions,' only movements of the water."

GOD IS AN OCEAN WITHOUT SHORES

Al-Hallaj

In the ecstasy of mystical union, the great 11th-century Sufi master al-Hallaj found himself announcing, "I am the Truth! I am God!" The Islamic authorities were appalled at his supposed blasphemy and had al-Hallaj crucified as a heretic. As the cross was prepared for him, he forgave his persecutors, saying:

"Lord forgive your servants who from religious zeal have gathered here to kill me. Have mercy on them, for if you had revealed to them what you have revealed to me, they would not be doing this. And if you had hidden from me what you have hidden from them, I would not have to suffer this. Glory to you, whatever you do and whatever you will."

Enlightened Saint or Egomaniac?

The greatest mystics and the greatest egotists have one thing in common – they both think they are God. So what is the difference? When the separate self thinks it is God, we have the deluded false prophet. When the separate self dissolves into God, we have the enlightened saint. A story told by the Sufis clarifies the difference between transcending the ego and inflating the ego.

One of the men who had crucified the Sufi saint al-Hallaj for declaring "I am God!" afterward had a dream. He was confused to see the heretical Sufi being ceremoniously taken up to heaven. He asked Allah, "Why was a pharaoh condemned for crying out 'I am God' and yet al-Hallaj is taken up to heaven for saying the same words?" Allah answered, "When the pharaoh spoke these words he thought only of himself and had forgotten Me. When al-Hallaj uttered these words – the same words – he had forgotten himself and thought only of Me. Therefore 'I am God' in the pharaoh's mouth was a curse to him, but in al-Hallaj's mouth this 'I am God' is the effect of My grace."

AN AWARENESS OF THE ONENESS

A simple spiritual practice that nurtures an awareness of mystical
Oneness is to consider the intrinsic interrelatedness of everything.

1 Sit quietly and let go of your habitual view of the world as made up of discrete separate things, allowing a vision of an ever-changing Whole to arise.

2 Contemplate the world around you. Consider how nothing in it could possibly exist in isolation. Without the sun, the plants would not have life. Without death and decay, there would be no new shoots. You would not exist without your ancestral lineage, stretching back through your human forebears to the first forms of life in the primal oceans and beyond to the formation of the universe itself. Nothing is separate. Everything functions as part of one all-embracing Totality.

3 Imagine all the separate things you can see, including your own body, as ripples on one great ocean of Being. See the world before you unfolding like some cosmic dance. Imagine all you hear as themes in one divine symphony.

4 Become aware of your thoughts, feelings, and sensations. They too are passing phenomena that exist only in relationship to other thoughts, feelings, and sensations. All things, including your own body and mind, are parts of the one universe. You are not a separate individual. You are Consciousness witnessing the constantly metamorphosing Oneness of Life.

5 If an awareness of the Oneness begins to arise, abandon thinking about it and just bathe in the sublime Unity.

BLACK ELK

❝ Peace comes within the souls of men when they realize their relationship, their Oneness, with the universe and all its powers; and when they realize that at the center of the universe dwells Great Spirit, and that this center is really everywhere. It is within each of us. ❞

BLACK ELK
NATIVE AMERICAN VISIONARY

❝ I must become God and God must become me, so completely that we share the same 'I' eternally. ❞

MEISTER ECKHART
CHRISTIAN SAGE

❝ The love and bliss of God are the primal state. Those who know they are not and act not refind themselves in the primal state of love and bliss. ❞

ABD AL-KADER
SUFI SAGE

❝ There is no 'I.' Nor is there anything 'other-than-I.' ❞

SENG T'SAN
ZEN MASTER

Living with the paradox

A S WE HAVE SEEN TIME *and again, spirituality is about being big enough to embrace paradox. We need to be detached, but we need to be fully here and now in the drama of life. We need to be self-disciplined, yet act spontaneously. We need to make our own effort, but also to realize that we do nothing. We need to differentiate good from bad, yet go beyond both. We need to think in new spiritual ways, yet to know that all thoughts are just concepts. We need to cultivate compassion and relieve suffering, but also to understand that everything is perfect just the way it is.*

WE ARE PARTS OF ONE WHOLE

WAVES ON THE OCEAN

All of these dilemmas stem from one great dilemma. We experience ourselves as separate bodies and personalities, but we are also indivisible parts of the Whole. Superficially we are individual waves which rise and fall on the one great ocean of Being, which is our deeper identity. Following the spiritual path is an ongoing process of attempting to resolve the great paradox of being a part of an indivisible Whole. How can this be done? The word "paradox" itself gives us a clue, coming as it does from the Greek *para dokien* – "beyond thought." The dilemma cannot be resolved by thinking about it. It is resolved in a profound acceptance of the fact that this is the way things are. A wave doesn't worry about being the ocean. It just IS.

THE IMPERSONAL "I"

The spiritual path is the process of discovering the impersonal sense of "I" that inhabits the personal sense of "me." Enlightenment is a sacred marriage between the "I" and the "me." It is living as God made flesh – both divine and human. It is about being in the world, but not of it. It is experiencing both com-union (with union) and com-passion (with passion). As the impersonal I, we experience communion with all that is in an all-embracing Oneness. As the personal me, we reach out with unconditional compassion to all the other separate beings confused and suffering in this strange world.

LIFE JUST IS WHAT IT IS

ENGAGED DETACHMENT

This exercise is a more subtle form of a contemplation exercise we have previously explored, which works with the metaphor of life being like a movie. It teaches us to be in the world but not of it; to balance being the detached impersonal Consciousness that witnesses life and also an engaged participant of the unfolding drama in the here and now.

Consider the best way of enjoying a movie. If you are so aware of the fact that you are merely watching an illusion on the screen, you will miss the whole experience. On the other hand, if you actually think you are the hero of the adventure, you will be completely terrified by the moments of suspense and danger, rather than enjoying them as an exciting part of the story. If, however, you enter into the illusion while retaining a tacit understanding that you are actually only the observer and no one is in reality living and dying, then you will be able to appreciate fully the drama without being overcome by it.

This is similar to the state of mind the saints and sages encourage us to adopt in relation to life. Most of us are so identified with the hero of our movie – the ego – that we need to concentrate on practices that cultivate detachment. Yet this can lead to a cold indifference, so we also need to enter into the tragicomedy of it all with heroic compassion in the face of life's suffering and a healthy sense of humor.

As you face the trials and tribulations of your daily existence, practice seeing life in this way. Once you have cultivated an attitude of engaged detachment, you will find that you can step in and out of life as required. When life is rich you can enjoy it without reservation, but when it becomes too painful you can remind yourselves that the "wicked witch" is only a passing fantasy that can in reality never touch you.

ENJOY LIFE AS IF IT WERE A MOVIE

" How can all things be One
yet each thing separate? "

PAGAN ORACLE OF ORPHEUS

❦❦❦❦

" Don't say 'I am nothing,'
but don't say 'I am something.'
Don't say 'Nothing concerns me,'
but don't say 'Something concerns me.'
Just say 'ALLAH' –
and you will witness wonders. "

SIDI ALI AL-JAMAL
SUFI SAGE

" When the human self
and the divine 'I' are interconnected
they can achieve perfection and eternity. "

VALENTINUS
GNOSTIC CHRISTIAN SAGE

" Inwardly be free of all hopes and desires,
but outwardly do what needs to be done.
Without hopes in your heart, live as if you were
full of hopes. Live with your heart now cool
and now warm, just like everyone else. Inwardly
give up the idea 'I am the doer,' yet outwardly
engage in all activities. This is how to live in the
world, completely free from the least trace of ego. "

MAHARAMAYANA
HINDU SCRIPTURE

BUDDHIST MONKS IN RYOANJI TEMPLE ROCK GARDEN, KYOTO, JAPAN

Conclusion

Fundamentally, the spiritual search is not motivated by the desire to be enlightened or merge with God. These sophisticated conceptual descriptions are much later accretions around a more primal pressure. The root motivation for becoming a spiritual seeker is that we need simply to feel good about life and death.

We all know that living can be a frightening, lonely, painful, grief-stricken ordeal. In the face of this, we desperately need to feel that in some way we are essentially safe.

We need to know that our joys and suffering have real meaning. Spirituality answers these needs. It frees us from the deep anxieties caused by believing ourselves to be isolated egos. It connects us to an immense benevolence that permeates creation, an unconditional compassion that beats the pulse of life, that Great Mystery that in reality we are. Those who dare to look beyond the limits of their habitual horizons and glimpse the infinite goodness that is God are forever reassured that all is well.

THE IRREPRESSIBLE POWER OF LIFE

PART FOUR

INFORMATION AT A GLANCE

Information that includes a glossary
of terms for easy reference, and a
list of further reading for those who
wish to explore spirituality further

Glossary

A

Age of Aquarius Approaching new astrological age determined by astronomical changes. The New Age movement takes its name from here.

Asceticism Self-denial and abstinence from worldly comforts and pleasures in order to evoke spiritual states of awareness.

Astral plane A different dimension of reality believed to be experienced during dreaming or meditation.

Atheism Belief that there is no God.

B

Buddhism Religion inspired by the Indian sage Siddhartha Gautama, who was known as Buddha. It teaches that man can achieve perfect enlightenment by transcending the ego-self.

C

Cabalism (Cabbalism, Kabbalism) Mystical Jewish sect which flourished in the Middle Ages. Uses the Cabala, also known as the Tree of Life, as a guide to achieving knowledge of God.

Chakras Energy centers in the body, specified by Indian yoga. There are seven chakras, which must be balanced for good health.

Christianity Monotheistic religion, with the central belief that Jesus Christ is the Son of God, who died to save mankind and will return to Earth on the Day of Judgement.

Cult A group with a particular ideology. In modern usage, the term tends to denote an organization with dubious ethics, sometimes one that exerts dictatorial demands on its followers.

F

Fundamentalism The interpretation of every word of a religion's sacred texts (for example the Bible) as literal truth. Fundamentalists tend to be hostile to other religious traditions.

G

Gnosticism Mystical early Christian sect that taught the need to experience "Gnosis" or direct Knowledge of God. Gnosticism was regarded as heresy and brutally eradicated by the Roman Church.

Great Spirit / Great Mystery Native American description of the Supreme Being.

Guru Hindu or Sikh religious teacher or leader, who gives guidance to his disciples.

H

Hari Krishna A mantra in praise of the Hindu god Krishna, famous for being sung by followers of the Krishna Consciousness Movement, founded by an Indian guru in the 1960s.

Hasidism A sect of Jewish mystics, known for their spiritual zeal and joy in worship.

Hinduism A general name for the broad spectrum of Indian cults, most of which worship many gods, but also acknowledge one Supreme Being known as Brahman.

I

Islam Monotheistic religion based on the teachings of the prophet Muhammad, which are contained in the holy scriptures of the Koran. Followers of Islam are called Muslims.

J

Judaism The religion of the Jews, which preaches that there is one God, and which is based on the Tanach (Old Testament) and the Talmud.

K

Karma Indian term for the idea that bad actions have a negative effect on fate, while good actions will be rewarded.

Koan Koans are used as an aid to meditation by certain Zen sects. They are mystical riddles that force the meditator to go beyond the rational mind.

M

Mantra Word or phrase repeated during meditation in order to block distracting thoughts and enter a mystical state of awareness.

Meditation Various techniques for stilling the mind and becoming aware of Consciousness itself.

Moonies (Unification Church) Cult formed by the Korean Reverend Sun Myung Moon, combining Christianity and traditional Korean beliefs. Moon claims to be the returning Christ.

Monism Belief that the fundamental reality is an impersonal Oneness. Taoism and Buddhism are monist philosophies.

Monotheism Belief that there is only one God. Judaism, Christianity, and Islam are monotheistic religions.

Mysticism A name for the perennial spiritual philosophy. Mysticism teaches that the supreme reality can not been known by thoughts, but only through direct experience. Mystics emphasize the underlying unity of all things, and recognize other religions as different ways of approaching the same truth.

N

New Age Movement encompassing various nontraditional forms of spirituality, alternative lifestyles, and therapies.

Nirvana The extinguishing of the separate self, leading to perfect enlightenment.

P

Paganism Polytheistic western religion, established in pre-Christian times, which included everything from shamanic nature worship to sophisticated mystical philosophy.

Peyote Central American hallucinogenic cactus, consumed as part of shamanic ritual.

Pilgrimage Journey to a place of especial religious significance, undertaken as a spiritual practice.

Polytheism Spiritual traditions, such as Shamanism, Hinduism, and ancient Paganism, that believe in many gods and goddesses, as well as ultimately acknowledging a supreme Oneness.

R

Retreat A place away from everyday distractions, where one can focus on spiritual practice.

Ritual death Simulation of death in order to confront deepest fears and overcome them.

S

Sacred Holy, consecrated. Exclusively devoted to a deity or a religious ceremony.

Scientology Cult founded by L. Ron Hubbard, based on popular psychology, occultism, and science fiction.

Shaman A "medicine man" or "witchdoctor" amongst the primal peoples, who communicates with the spirit world by entering altered states of awareness, achieved by means of sacred rituals or psychedelic power plants.

Shamanism Ancient spiritual tradition based on the belief that the world is full of spirits that make life possible, and which in return get their sustenance from human ritual and prayer.

Siddhis Indian word for magical powers, such as levitation and reading the mind.

Sikhism Indian sect derived from Hinduism, founded by Guru Nanak. Its holy book is the Guru Granth.

Smudging Purification method first used by Native Americans, to prepare oneself and one's sacred space for spiritual practice. Sacred herbs are burned and the smoke wafted about.

Sufism Mystical Muslim sect believing that we are all part of God, and that the individual self is only an illusion.

Sweat lodge Place where purification is achieved through a steam bath. A traditional ritual of Native Americans.

T

Tai Chi Chuan Chinese martial art, used as a form of exercise to achieve flexibility and strength. The Chinese believe that "chi" is an invisible life force, which exists in the body in various forms. Tai chi promotes the flow of chi around the body.

Tantric sex Tantrism is an Indian yoga that sometimes uses sexuality as a way of worshipping God.

Taoism Ancient Chinese spiritual philosophy whose most famous spokesperson is the legendary sage Lao Tzu. It advocates living in harmony with Tao – the flow of life.

Theosophy The name of an eclectic mystical movement set up by Madame Helena Blavatsky.

Tibetan Book of the Dead Tibetan scripture read out loud to the dying to prepare them for entry to the next world.

V

Vedas Sacred writings of Hinduism. The oldest scriptures of humankind.

Vision Quest Native American spiritual practice involving isolation in a wild, natural environment, in order to commune with nature and confront fears.

Visualization Form of meditation using the power of the imagination to communicate with the unconscious mind. Simple forms of visualization are used as an aid to relaxation.

W

Wu Wei State of being which is cultivated in Taoism, when a harmony with existence is achieved which includes no sense of being a separate individual.

Y

Yin and Yang Chinese names for the fundamental polarity of existence. Yin and Yang are opposites, yet interdependent; relative, and always in transition.

Yoga Indian system of exercise that works towards flexibility, and harmony between mind and body.

Yogas Spiritual paths to achieving enlightenment, taught in Hinduism. The most important yogas are Bhakti and Gnana.

Z

Zen Chinese fusion of Buddhism and Taoism, which flourished in Japan. It emphasizes the need for direct experience of the fundamental nature of reality.

Further Reading

I am often asked to recommend books on spirituality, but so many wonderful books have been written over the centuries that it is impossible to provide a definitive list of the best works. Let me mention, however, a few of my favorites (and some of my own works), which I regularly point people toward.

For accessible, profound, and beautifully light-hearted insights, check out the books and taped talks of the American teacher Ram Dass. I have also found the works of the Vietnamese Zen Master Thich Nhat Hanh to be deep and lucid. For a profoundly philosophical approach to spirituality I love the works of Ramesh Balsekar and his master Sri Nisargadatta Maharaj. For an ancient classic full of enigmatic wisdom, puzzle over Lao Tzu's *Tao Te Ching* – there are many good versions among which I count my own.

For a deeper understanding of the mystical heart of all religions, take a look at *The Perennial Philosophy* by Aldous Huxley. You could also try *The Complete Guide to World Mysticism*, which I wrote with my spiritual brother Peter Gandy. I have also written a series of little books called *The Wisdom of the World*, which collect some remarkable insights from the great saints and sages of different traditions. In *The Illustrated Book of Sacred Scriptures* I explore the same core teachings as expressed in holy texts.

For general inspiration I personally turn to mystical poetry. I am particularly fed by the ecstatic love-poems of Jalal al-Din Rumi, the raving excesses of Walt Whitman and the sublime density of T. S. Eliot, especially The Four Quartets. If you are looking for an exciting read that will completely revolutionize your understanding of Christianity, I must finally suggest you dive into *The Jesus Mysteries – Was the Original Jesus a Pagan God?* the groundbreaking bestseller by Peter Gandy and me.

In my own experience, to find the next book I should read I rely on what Carl Jung called the "Library Angel" – that strange magic whereby you are irresistibly drawn to a particular cover for no apparent reason, or the right book falls off of a shelf onto your head. I hope the Library Angel leads you to your next source of spiritual nourishment. Enjoy your journey and live an extraordinary life.

Timothy Freke 1999

Index

Picture credits

Archiv für kunst und Geschichte, London: 12, 15L, 22b, 22t, 25, 27, 32b, 46, 55, 83, 106, 134, 160/161, 179 (Musée d'Orsay) 209, 210/211, 213, 224/225, 233.

The Bridgeman Art Library, London: 17t and 20b (Victoria & Albert Museum), 23 (Christies), 68, 98b, 103, 115r (Oriental Museum, Durham), 125 (National Museum Delhi), 130/131, 137t, 154, 155, 163, 179, 203.
BAL/Giraudon: 191.

Corbis, London: 37t, 45, 46t, 74t, 114, 116, 119, 128t, 129b, 147, 194, 208t, 220, 221, 244.

Hulton-Getty: 151.

The Hutchison Library: 16, 19b and 204/205 (Melanie Friend), 34/35 and 102b (Patricio Goycolea), 47 (Paul Massey), 48/49, 62t and 133 (Michael Macintyre), 66b and 108t (Robin Constable), 28br (Jon Wright), 129t and 130t (Brian Moser), 71b (Carlos Freire), 176 (Ian Lloyd).

The Image Bank, London: 52, 54, 64t, 64b, 115t, 122bl, 123t, 159, 162, 170, 170t, 177, 190, 210, 234b, 238b, 242, 243.

The Stock Market, London: 30, 59, 99, 101, 104/105, 109, 113, 124b, 133, 150, 152, 175, 186t, 200t, 219, 243.

NASA: 48t, 206.

Nick Woods/Sacred Hoop Magazine: 110b.

Courtesy Robert Natkin: 37b, 168, 199.

Rex Features, London: 26b, 42/43, 43, 44, 53, 60/61, 112l, 132b, 141, 145b, 180t.

Tony Stone Associates: 33, 56/57, 79r, 117, 204, 228b, 232, 245.

Trip/Art Directors: 18, 28b, 71, 75t, 75b, 100b, 102t, 120b, 122bl, 142/143, 143t, 190, 198, 211.